CLEOPATRA'S NEEDLES

CLEOPATRA'S NEEDLES

R A Hayward

MOORLAND PUBLISHING COMPANY

ISBN 0 903485 82 6

Photoset by Advertiser Printers Ltd, Newton Abbot
and printed in Great Britain
by Redwood Burn Ltd, Trowbridge & Esher
for Moorland Publishing Company
The Market Place, Hartington, Buxton, Derbyshire SK17 0AL

Contents

Illustrations

Acknowledgements

The author wishes to record his gratitude to the staffs of the various libraries visited while researching this book, for the willingness with which they made books and other material available, and for the excellence of the photographic illustrations they provided. In particular his thanks go to the Library of the University of Keele, the Manchester Central Reference Library, the John Rylands University Library of Manchester, and the North Staffordshire Polytechnic. Without their help and co-operation this book could not have been written. Last, but by no means least, the author acknowledges the role played by his wife Shirley, not only in typing the manuscript, but in her patient support and understanding.

The author and publisher are grateful to the following for the use of illustrations: Mary Evans Picture Library: Figs 23, 31, 46, 63; The Museum of London: Figs 27, 28, 44, 45; National Maritime Museum, London: Figs 22, 24, 26; Radio Times Hulton Picture Library: Figs 2, 6, 7, 13, 15, 33, 48, 58, 65.

Introduction

During the nineteenth century three large obelisks were taken from Egypt and erected in Paris, London, and New York, as monuments to the grandeur and achievements of the civilisation created by the ancient Egyptians. Over three thousand years earlier the mightiest warrior of all the pharaohs, Thothmes III, commanded that a pair of obelisks be carved out of the rose-red granite of the Aswan area of Upper Egypt. These were erected at Heliopolis to adorn the entrance of the great Temple of the Sun, and there they remained upright and aloof through centuries of dramatic change right down to the dawn of the Christian era. Then these gigantic single-stone columns were removed to Alexandria and re-erected at the Caesareum, a palace which stood on the shores of the Mediterranean. Nearly two thousand years later this pair of obelisks, by now popularly referred to as Cleopatra's Needles, were on the move again, but this time they parted company, one bound for London while its twin companion was destined to cross the Atlantic Ocean to take up residence in New York.

At some unrecorded date the British needle had toppled to the ground, and over the centuries it had slowly been covered by the drifting sand. In 1820 the ruler of Egypt, Mehemet Ali, presented it to Britain to mark the Coronation of King George IV. However, for another fifty years the prostrate needle slumbered on undisturbed in its sandy grave, since the British Government could not make up its mind about what to do with the gift; and in any case it was reluctant to bear the expense of bringing the obelisk to England. This apparent indifference to the Cleopatra's Needle, and the glories of the civilisation it represented, was neatly summed up in a contemporary article which commented rather sarcastically that England appeared 'to be in the position of the elderly lady who won an elephant in a lottery'. The French meanwhile had also become the owners of an Egyptian obelisk, and at an enormous cost they transported their huge monolith to Paris where in 1836 they proudly raised it in the Place de la Concorde. Despite the humiliation of having her old enemy showing her how it should be done, the British Government were unimpressed about the virtue of decorating the capital with a relic of ancient Egyptian craftsmanship, and in the end it was left to the enterprise of certain private individuals to promote the venture.

In 1867 General Sir James Alexander mounted a determined campaign to persuade the British Government to rescue her Cleopatra's Needle from the sands of Egypt. For nearly ten years he battled unsuccessfully to try and convince the authorities of the merits of the plan, before reluctantly deciding there was no alternative but to appeal to the patriotism of his countrymen for help in promoting what he passionately believed to be a national duty.

Thanks to Alexander's efforts the eminent surgeon Erasmus Wilson offered to finance the project, and the task of carrying out this novel venture was entrusted to the civil engineer John Dixon. Right from the start the undertaking was fraught with difficulty, but eventually after numerous setbacks the obelisk had been safely encased in a purpose built cylindrical iron barge which was aptly christened *Cleopatra.* In September 1877 she was towed out of Alexandria harbour by the British merchantman *Olga* en route to England. Four weeks later the *Cleopatra's* ballast shifted during a severe storm in the Bay of Biscay, and she heeled right over onto her starboard beam ends. Tragically six seamen were drowned, and Captain Carter was forced to abandon his stricken vessel to the mercy of the elements. When all hope of saving the *Cleopatra* had faded, the *Olga* continued her voyage alone and bore the sad tidings to England. The attempt to grace London with the presence of an Egyptian obelisk did not end there, for Dixon persevered until he had completed his mission.

It is now just one hundred years since John Dixon raised his obelisk on the Thames Embankment. To celebrate the centenary of this memorable event the chapters which follow describe the obelisk's chequered career and relate the saga of the various attempts to persuade the British Government to bring the Cleopatra's Needle to London. Detailed accounts are also given of the tragic tale of the *Cleopatra*, and of the trials and tribulations which beset John Dixon and his fellow engineers before they finally triumphed. A brief account is also given of the erection of the Luxor Obelisk in Paris by LeBas, and a chapter is devoted to the story of the British needle's twin sister which was presented by the Khedive of Egypt to the City of New York in 1879. Despite strenuous opposition to its removal, Lieutenant-Commander Henry Gorringe of the US Navy resolutely overcame all the obstacles facing him, and within less than two years had succeeded in transporting his Cleopatra's Needle across the Atlantic and erecting it in Central Park.

1

Egyptian Obelisks

The ancient Egyptians were skilled craftsmen, and the works they created in stone range from small delicately carved figures to one of the seven wonders of the world, the Pyramids, which still rank high amongst the largest of man-made structures. They also erected large single-stone obelisks, two of which—the so called Cleopatra's Needles—were erected at the command of Pharaoh Thothmes III around 1450BC, a thousand years after Cheops commissioned the Great Pyramid of Giza. An obelisk is a four sided pillar which tapers gently upwards from the base to terminate in a small pyramid or pyramidion. Its four sides are usually inscribed with hieroglyphics recording the name and achievements of the pharaoh responsible for its erection. Although other ancient civilisations erected stone columns, the obelisk appears to have been a peculiarly Egyptian form of monolith, and the earliest examples date from well before 2000BC. Obelisks vary enormously in size, ranging from tiny specimens a few inches high to giants over one hundred feet tall weighing many hundreds of tons. Most of the larger obelisks were quarried from the rose-red granite, or syrenite, of the Aswan area of Upper Egypt.

In the nineteenth century obelisks were taken from Egypt and re-erected in Paris, London, and New York, and the engineers concerned faced great difficulties in completing their tasks due to the sheer size and weight of these single-stone columns. How then did the ancient Egyptians, with only fairly basic engineering skills at their disposal, manage to quarry these enormous stones, move them across rough ground to the Nile, transport them hundreds of miles downriver, and finally erect them? The question cannot be answered satisfactorily, for many of the secrets of the Egyptian engineers have been lost in the mists of time. A clue does exist as to how they were quarried, for a gigantic uncompleted specimen lies on its side in the quarry at Aswan. The obelisk is still attached to the bedrock, having been abandoned due to fissures in the stone when the work was well advanced. The top surface and sides of this huge stone have been roughly shaped, and had it been completed it would have been a veritable giant among obelisks for it weighs over one thousand tons. After masons had finished dressing the three sides of an obelisk roughly to size, it would then have been separated from the bedrock, probably by the use of wedges, turned over, and the remaining side dressed. The ancient Egyptians relied upon a power source denied to modern men, the muscles of thousands of slaves, who, straining on ropes and manning large levers, would laboriously hoist the slender but heavy monolith out of the quarry. Then, probably mounted on a timber sled, it was by dint of human sweat dragged down to the River Nile, its progress over the rough terrain perhaps being eased by wooden rollers or even a carpet of sand. Alternatively it may have been continually tipped

1 The Karnak Obelisks. Two of the many obelisks erected by the ancient Egyptians. The one on the right was set up around 1,520BC by Thothmes I, and its companion a few years later by Queen Hatshepsut, wife of Thothmes III — the pharaoh responsible for the erection of the so-called Cleopatra's Needles.(From *Egypt* by G. Ebers).

2 The Aswan Obelisk. This gigantic specimen lies uncompleted in the quarry at Aswan, work on it having been abandoned due to fissures in the granite.

over on its side by long levers to roll its way slowly to the river, but this is pure conjecture. For the passage down the Nile a large flat bottomed boat or a raft must have been employed, and under the control of a fleet of small craft the seasonal flood waters may have borne on its way as they swept down to the Delta to bring life to the fertile soil. Once the obelisk reached its destination how was it raised into the vertical position? This is perhaps the most intriguing question of all, and various theories have been put forward. Maybe it was hauled up a ramp and carefully lowered off the end, but the actual system used by these ancient engineers, who triumphed time and again in performing their stupendous feats, is unfortunately shrouded in mystery, although one factor in their success is certain, namely the Pharaoh's ability as the whim took him to summon unlimited manpower.

The boundaries of the Pharaoh's domain fluctuated over the centuries as first one, then another, of her neighbours encroached upon the frontiers, only to be temporarily pushed back by the Egyptians. The greatest warrior of all the Egyptian kings was Thothmes III,

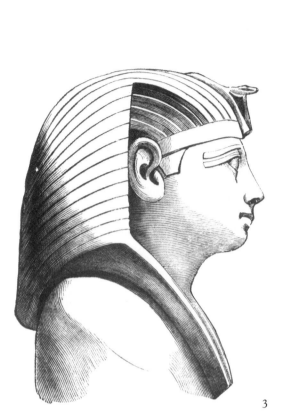

3

4

one of the fourteen pharaohs who ruled during the XVIIIth Dynasty. During his reign, circa 1500-1450BC, Thothmes fought no fewer than seventeen campaigns and extended Egypt's influence northeastwards across Syria to the River Euphrates, and southwards into the Sudan as far as the fourth cateract of the Nile. Among the many buildings and monuments erected in his name were a pair of red granite obelisks which stood like sentinels at the entrance to the great Temple of the Sun at Heliopolis (the Biblical city of On) just north of the site of modern Cairo on the east bank of the Nile. Over three thousand years later this pair of obelisks were destined to part company, and one now graces the Thames Embankment in London while its companion stands on a knoll in New York's Central Park. Each obelisk towers almost seventy feet high above its pedestal and weighs over one hundred and eighty tons. After their erection at Heliopolis, the skilled Egyptian masons inscribed a single column of hieroglyphics down the centre of each tapering side to record the name and attributes of Thothmes III. Two hundred years and eleven pharaohs later these inscriptions were flanked by more hieroglyphics extolling the virtues of Ramses II, another mighty warrior who vanquished the Hittites.

The story now moves forward some twelve centuries, almost to the dawn of the Christian era. The Egyptian civilisation had long since fallen from its pre-eminent position, and after being subjugated in turn by the Ethiopians, the Persians, and the Greeks under Alexander the Great, Egypt was ruled for three hundred years by the Ptolemaic Dynasty. Alexandria, on the Mediterranean coast of Egypt, was founded in 332BC by Alexander the Great, and under the rule of Ptolemies it became the cultural centre of the world, renowned for its art, science, and learning, and famous for its library,

14

3 Pharaoh Thothmes III. The mightiest warrior of all the pharaohs, he ruled Egypt about 1,500-1,450BC. Thothmes commissioned the pair of red granite obelisks which later became popularly known as the Cleopatra's Needles.(From *Cleopatra's Needle* by J. King).

4 Pharaoh Ramses II. Renowned for vanquishing the Hittites around 1,280BC. Ramses added further hieroglyphic inscriptions to the Cleopatra's Needles.(From *Cleopatra's Needle* by J. King).

5 Queen Cleopatra. A bas-relief now in the British Museum. She was the last ruler of the Ptolemaic Dynasty. Cleopatra achieved notoriety for her love affairs with Julius Caesar and Mark Antony. She committed suicide in 30BC.*(The Graphic,* 1878).

5

museum, and other great buildings. After the death in 30BC of Queen Cleopatra, the last of the Ptolemies, Egypt became part of the Roman Empire. The pair of obelisks erected at Heliopolis by Thothmes III had proudly stood for fifteen centuries unconcerned by all these changes, but now they were taken down and brought to Alexandria. Here the architect Pontius raised them at the Water Gate of the Caesareum, a palace on the edge of the Mediterranean commissioned by Cleopatra in memory of one of her lovers, Julius Caesar. Centuries later the two obelisks were popularly referred to as the Cleopatra's Needles, although by then no one was quite sure as to when they had been erected at Alexandria. In 1877 a young English engineer, Waynman Dixon (who was to play an important role in shipping one of the needles to Britain), discovered conclusive proof that the two obelisks were set up at Alexandria eighteen years after the death of Cleopatra during the reign of the Roman Emperor Augustus. Whether they were brought from Heliopolis on the Queen's instructions is not known, and it has been suggested that the nickname Cleopatra's Needles arose from their shape and the relationships Cleopatra, surely the most infamous of all Alexandria's residents, formed with Julius Caesar and Mark Antony.

The Romans removed many obelisks from Egypt, and quite naturally most of these trophies ended up in Rome where eventually well over a dozen decorated the capital of the empire. The Emperor Augustus transported two at the same time in an enormous vessel specially constructed for the purpose, and they were put in the Circus Maximus and Campus Martius. Other emperors followed his example including Caligula, Claudius, and Constantine. In 1586, at the order of Pope Sixtus V, the obelisk brought to Rome by

6 The Vatican Obelisk. Domenico Fontana removing the obelisk from the Circus of Nero in order to re-erect it in St Peters Square.

Caligula was carefully lifted off its pedestal and lowered to the ground in preparation for re-erecting it nearby in St Peter's Square facing the Vatican. The work was supervised by the famous architect Domenico Fontana, who with the aid of nearly one thousand men and 140 horses successfully completed the whole operation in under six months. The obelisk was raised aloft using a forest of timber scaffolding, popularly referred to as 'Fontana's Castle', and a web of ropes which led to forty capstans manned by his army of workmen. The Vatican Obelisk weighs around 330 tons, stands 85 feet high, and, unusually, its sides are free from hieroglyphic inscription. This probably explains the Pope's desire to see it standing in front of the Vatican, for he incongruously turned it into a Christian monument by mounting a large cross on top of the pyramidion.

For fifteen hundred years the two Cleopatra's Needles stood side by side on the Alexandrian shore as the Caesareum slowly crumbled around them, its end hastened by the sea which relentlessly eroded the foundations. Then, at some unrecorded date, one of the needles toppled to the ground to be slowly covered by the drifting sand. The reason for its fall is uncertain. Perhaps one of the earthquakes which struck the eastern Mediterranean in the sixteenth century was responsible, or maybe it was the work of metal thieves who had coveted the four bronze supports on which the Romans had mounted each obelisk. One thing is certain, the needle fell before 1610, for in that year the traveller George Sandys noted that it was lying prostrate and half buried.

In July 1798 French troops landed in Egypt and seized it from the Turks; however, Napoleon Bonaparte was thwarted in his ambition to conquer the Middle East, and ultimately India, by the bravery and enterprise of British sailors and soldiers. As a necessary preliminary to her invasion of Egypt, France had captured Malta and had virtually succeeded in driving the Royal Navy out of the Mediterranean. With British fortunes at a low ebb, and morale sapped by the Spithead Mutiny of the previous year, a squadron of warships commanded by Horatio Nelson entered the Mediterranean to scour the inland sea for the French fleet. On 1 August 1798 he found his quarry lying at anchor in Aboukir Bay, fifteen miles east of Alexandria. Nelson was faced with a numerically stronger adversary, but undaunted he daringly led his fifteen ships against the French fleet at sunset. The Battle of the Nile raged all night, and resulted in a crushing defeat for the

16

French. On land France had quickly defeated the Turks, but when her victorious army advanced into Syria they were ejected by a force commanded by Sir Sydney Smith. For three years France fought to retain her control of Egypt, but fate ordained otherwise. In March 1801 General Ralph Abercromby landed at Aboukir Bay with 15,000 British troops to be met on the beach with strong opposition from French dragoons who charged out of the sand dunes. After fierce fighting the French withdrew towards Alexandria, and a series of skirmishes followed as the British force slowly advanced along the coast. The decisive battle, the Battle of Alexandria, was fought on 21 March within sight of the standing Cleopatra's Needle. For a while the fighting see-sawed back and forth, but eventually General Menou, who was outnumbered two to one, retreated to fortifications in the city. Losses were high on both sides, and regrettably they included General Abercromby, who, before the battle was finally won, fell mortally wounded. A few months later surrender terms were negotiated and the garrisons at Alexandria and Cairo capitulated, thus ending the French occupation of Egypt. Most of the British troops were soon withdrawn and the

7 The Vatican Obelisk standing in front of St Peters, Rome. Incongruously the Pope turned it into a Christian monument by mounting a cross on top of the pyramidion.

8 The Cleopatra's Needles in 1737. A Danish naval captain, Frederick Lewis Norden, visited the two obelisks which were situated just outside the ruined walls of Old Alexandria. Only the butt of the fallen needle was visible and due to the angle at which it jutted out of the sand, Norden wrongly concluded that it had been broken in its fall.(F. L. Norden, *Travels in Egypt and Nubia*).

9 Death of Sir Ralph Abercromby. General Abercromby fell mortally wounded in March 1801 at the Battle of Alexandria. The first attempt to bring the prostrate Cleopatra's Needle to Britain followed shortly afterwards; the object was to provide a memorial to the British victories over the French and to the price paid by the gallant Abercromby and many of his countrymen for the liberation of Egypt.(*The Graphic*, 1878).

country was handed back to the Turks, but a small contingent was left behind under the command of the Earl of Cavan.

The French had apparently intended taking the two Cleopatra's Needles home as trophies, for the sand around the fallen needle had been cleared away, and a cable attached to the top of its companion in preparation for pulling it down. This gave Cavan the idea of bringing the prostrate obelisk to Britain and erecting it as a memorial to the British victories and the price paid by Abercromby and so many of his countrymen for the liberation of Egypt. The Turks readily granted permission for the needle to be removed, so Cavan set to with a will. One of the officers concerned in the project takes up the story.

Having conferred with our Chief Engineer on the spot, namely, Major Bryce...the plan for the embarkation and conveyance to England of the fallen "Needle of Cleopatra" was prepared, and, upon due consideration, adopted.

The troops then remaining in Egypt were invited by their Officers to subscribe a certain number of days' pay to meet the Expenses of an undertaking in which their feelings were deeply interested, an invitation which was eagerly accepted, so that Lord Cavan instantly found the necessary funds for his purpose at his disposal. Officers, Non-Commissioned Officers, and Soldiers vied with each other in offering their Contributions to the furtherance of an object so gratifying to their National and their Professional pride, and the work was forthwith put in progress, in the following manner; One of the largest of the French Frigates *(El Corso)* captured at Alexandria was purchased, of the Prize Agents, from the Funds thus contributed, to convey the fallen Needle to England. A Stone Pier or jetty was commenced, alongside of which, when completed, the Frigate was to be brought, to receive the needle, which was to be introduced into the Ship on Rollers, through a Stern Port to be cut to the necessary size, and when introduced, was to be laid upon a Bed of large Blocks of Timber, forming a platform upon the Keel of the ship, so as to keep this immense weight of solid substance exactly amidships, and to prevent its straining the Keel. Thus placed in the hold of the Ship, the Needle was to be secured in its bed, so as to preclude the possibility of its being moved therefrom by the motion of the Ship at Sea. As the fallen Needle lay close to the Sea, the moving it upon Rollers from where it lay, to the Ship, became a very easy operation.

Matters being thus arranged, the necessary Working Parties were allotted daily, in the general orders issued by M.-Genl. the Earl of Cavan, and the undertaking proceeded most prosperously. To compensate the soldiery for the tear and wear of their Necessaries, Working Pay was issued to the Working Parties from the Funds which they themselves had contributed.

Considerable progress was made with the Jetty, and the Superior Officers of the Royal Navy then at Alexandria, viz. Captains Larcom and Donelly, embarked most zealously and cordially in our project, which must therefore have been perfectly successful, had it not been abandoned, in consequence of orders received from Lord Keith and General Fox, who at the time held the chief Command of the Fleet and of the Troops serving in the Mediterranean.[1]

The contract with the Prize Agents for *El Corso* was cancelled, and the unused portion of the funds was returned to the subscribers. Later *The Graphic* pondered upon the reasons why this commendable plan to commemorate the British victories should have been cancelled, and perhaps there is more than a grain of truth in its conclusions, that 'Fox trembled for the discipline of his soldiers and the pipeclay on their regimentals. Lord Keith deemed such services unbecoming the Navy, not to speak of his misgivings as to what might happen if the ship should founder.'[2]

With transporting the obelisk to England out of the question, Cavan decided that some sort of memorial must be provided in Egypt, so after consulting his senior officers a suitably worded bronze plaque was engraved. To protect it from thieves, and those who at a later date might wish to deface it—for allegiances are often short lived—the plaque was buried for safety beneath the pedestal of the fallen obelisk. Years later is was brought back to England, and it is now mounted in a place of honour on the wall of the officers' mess at Mandora Barracks, Aldershot.

In 1805 Mehemet Ali Pasha became ruler of Egypt, and conscious of the debt his country owed to Britain, and in gratitude for gifts received, in 1811 he turned to the British Consul, Samuel Briggs, for advice as to what might be an acceptable present for King George III.

I was encouraged to submit to His Highness [Mehemet Ali] my opinion that one of the obelisks at Alexandria, known in Europe under the appellation of Cleopatra's Needles, might possibly be acceptable to His Majesty, as unique of its kind in England.... His Highness promised to take the subject into consideration; and, since my return to England, I have received a letter from his Minister, authorising me, if I deemed it acceptable, to make, in his master's name, a tender of one of those obelisks to his Majesty, as a mark of his personal respect and gratitude.[3]

Mehemet Ali's decision was rather belated, for it was not made until 1820, and his action was probably prompted by a desire to mark the accession of King George IV to the throne. The offer aroused widespread interest in Britain, and the concensus of public opinion was that the fallen obelisk should be brought to England as it would not be proper to remove its standing partner. A proposal was made that the needle should be erected in Waterloo

20

10 Mehemet Ali, (1769-1849). A high-ranking Turkish army officer who in 1805 was elected ruler of Egypt. Under his guidance the country took its first steps towards separate nationhood, although for many years after Mehemet Ali's death Egypt remained part of the Ottoman Empire. In 1841 he became the hereditary ruler of Egypt, and his family retained power for over a century until the overthrow of King Farouk.(From *Egypt* by G. Ebers).

Place, opposite Carlton House, where George IV had lived when Prince of Wales. However, when the cost of transporting and erecting the obelisk in London was estimated at £15,000, the British Government were less than enthusiastic about spending such a large sum of money on the acquisition of just one antiquity. Two years later a naval captain, William Henry Smyth, drew up detailed plans for the operation, and Mehemet Ali is reported to have offered to build a pier adjacent to the Cleopatra's Needle so that it could be loaded aboard a ship. Although the government gave some consideration to Smyth's proposal, they did nothing towards implementing it. In fact when Captain Smyth called upon a Minister to discuss his plans for erecting the obelisk as a monument to the British triumphs in Egypt, he was rebuffed with the insensitive comment 'Oh! I dare say Chantrey will cut us one in Aberdeenshire for less money than it would cost to bring the other away.'[4] In 1831, on the Coronation of William IV, Mehemet Ali renewed his offer and said that if Britain would send a ship he would put the obelisk on board her free of charge, but again no action was taken.

Meanwhile the Egyptian Government had offered the upright Cleopatra's Needle to

France, an act which aroused great indignation in Britain, not only amongst antiquaries, but more so in military circles. Britain had saved Egypt from French domination, and it seemed inconceivable that Mehemet Ali's memory could be so short. Yet now he was favouring his country's oppressor by presenting her with the spoils of war, as though France, and not Britain, had been the victor. Then to crown it all, Mehemet Ali committed what many people regarded as an act of barbarism. The French expressed a preference for the better preserved obelisks at Luxor, the only pair surviving erect in their original settings, and Mehemet Ali obligingly told them to help themselves to whichever one they wished.

In 1829 the French began constructing a ship at the Mediterranean port of Toulon in order to transport their Luxor Obelisk to Paris. The *Louqsor* was equipped with a removable bow to facilitate loading her valuable cargo. In April 1831 she left for Egypt manned by a crew of 132 men, and after sailing over five hundred miles up the Nile arrived at Thebes, one mile from Luxor, three months later. The whole operation was to be carried out under the supervision of a naval engineer, Jean Baptiste LeBas. His first task was to construct an inclined plane from the chosen obelisk to the river bank. It took 800 labourers, working fourteen hours a day, barely four months to cut through two huge rubbish tips, flatten part of a village, and grade the 500 yard long incline. This was quite an achievement, for the work was hampered by an outbreak of cholera which claimed the lives of fifteen Frenchmen and innumerable Egyptian labourers. The obelisk, meanwhile, had been covered with wooden planking to protect the hieroglyphics from damage. Using ten huge timber sheers, or masts, and ropes and capstans, LeBas carefully lowered the obelisk, and by 19 December 1831 he had succeeded in hauling it to the foot of the incline. Within less than a fortnight it had been safely embarked through the gaping bow of the *Louqsor*. The operation had been badly timed, for by the time the vessel was ready to depart, the river was too low for the passage back down to the Mediterranean, and it was not until New Year's Day 1833 that she finally reached Alexandria. The captain of the *Louqsor* appears to have had very little confidence in the sea-going qualities of his ship, for he waited three months in the shelter of Alexandria harbour before venturing out into the open sea for the voyage to Paris. Having stopped for a while in Gibraltar, the *Louqsor* eventually sailed up the River Seine in December 1833, after a slow but uneventful voyage, and she was then

11 The Paris Obelisk. LeBas raising the Luxor obelisk in the Place de la Concorde in October 1836 before a huge crowd.(*The Graphic*, 1878).

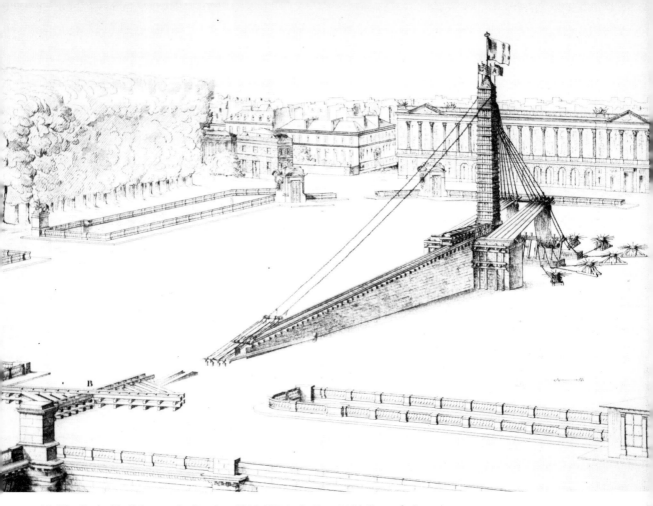

12 The Paris Obelisk erect in October 1836.(J.B.A. LeBas, *L'Obelisque de Luxor*).

moored alongside the Place de la Concorde. There she remained until the following August when the obelisk was disembarked by 240 artillerymen. The re-erection process was carried out in a similar manner to the lowering at Luxor. A long ramp was built, and the obelisk mounted on a sled was dragged up it on rails using five large capstans manned by 300 men who obeyed a system of trumpet calls give by LeBas. To ease its passage up the incline hot grease was repeatedly poured onto the wooden rails to reduce friction. The final operation of pulling the obelisk erect took place in October 1836 before a huge crowd estimated at 200,000 people. Ten masts, five each side, some 70 feet high and 18 inches diameter were used, together with a complicated system of ropes and pulley blocks, iron chains, and ten capstans each manned by a crew of forty-eight men. Among the vast crowd assembled to witness this historical event was an English architect, George Godwin, who recorded his impressions on this final phase of LeBas's mission.

It was about half-past eleven in the morning when the first signal was given and the capstans put in motion, and in less than ten minutes the end of the obelisk had described an arc of 10ft. At this moment a slight crash was heard, and the operations were immediately suspended. As may be easily imagined, the feelings of anxiety and excitement which pervaded the breast of all the immense multitude assembled became intense in the extreme; but after the expiration of an hour, during which time additional precautions were taken, the capstans were again put in motion, and without the least oscillation the immense mass was gradually raised into its present situation, where, as a French architect writes, it will probably remain until some terrific convulsion of our globe occurs to displace it.[5]

The swinging operation had taken just under three hours to complete, less than a quarter of the time needed by Fontana in 1586 to erect the Vatican Obelisk, and LeBas had used far less manpower. The Luxor Obelisk is somewhat smaller than its cousin in Rome, with a weight of around 250 tons and a height of 77 feet. All told, from beginning to end, the work had taken seven years, and had cost the staggering sum of £80,000. LeBas was well rewarded for his feat by a grateful French Government, for he received a bonus of 4000 francs, the Legion of Honour, and the appointment of Director of the Naval Museum.

In 1832 the question of bringing the prostrate Cleopatra's Needle to England was raised in the House of Commons by a member of the opposition, Joseph Hume, who pleaded in vain for the government to follow the example set by France. From time to time the subject cropped up, for instance around 1840 in connection with the laying out of Trafalgar Square. It was suggested that the obelisk should be erected there as a centre piece, but in the event its place was taken by the familiar Nelson's Column. Of course not everyone was enthusiastic about the Cleopatra's Needle. Most people were completely indifferent to it, and a few were positively antagonistic. One such was William Makepeace Thackeray, author of *Vanity Fair, Pendennis,* and other popular Victorian novels, who also wrote

13 The Paris Obelisk standing proudly in the Place de la Concorde. It weighs about 250 tons and towers 77 feet high above its pedestal.

under the pseudonym Michael Angelo Titmarsh. In the mid 1840s he visited Egypt, and like many another tourist went to inspect the obelisk. He later wrote:

The huge shaft lies on the ground prostrate, and desecrated by all sorts of abominations. Children were sprawling about, attracted by the dirt there. Arabs, negroes, and donkey boys were passing, quite indifferent, by the fallen monster of a stone—as indifferent as the British Government, who don't care for recording the glorious termination of their Egyptian campaign of 1801. If our country takes the compliment so coolly, surely it would be disloyal upon our part to be more enthusiastic. I wish they would offer the Trafalgar Square Pillar to the Egyptians; and that both of the huge, ugly monsters, were lying in the dirt there, side by side.[6]

Interest in the subject seemed to wane, although occasionally it was referred to in items published in the newspapers and journals, and once or twice questions were asked in Parliament. Then in April 1849 the Whig Government announced their intention of bringing the needle back to Britain. As before the cost was estimated at £15,000. Public interest was once more aroused and several possible locations for setting it up in London were considered. However, after heeding the advice of the eminent Egyptologist, Sir Gardner Wilkinson, the plans were shelved. Wilkinson later commented that the 'project has been wisely abandoned; and cooler deliberation has pronounced that, from its mutilated state, and the obliteration of many of the hieroglyphics by exposure to the sea air, it is unworthy the expense of removal.'[7] Two years later the position was reconsidered when the economist Joseph Hume again pressed the government to carry out the project. He was supported in the House of Lords by Lord Westmeath, who was told the matter was under consideration. A revised estimate of £7,000 was prepared, but the Whigs were unwilling to provide the necessary money. In 1853 the Sydenham Crystal Palace Company obtained permission to embellish the Egyptian Court of their exhibition with the obelisk, then unfortunately they had second thoughts about the commercial viability of the Cleopatra's Needle as an attraction. So it went on, plans came and went, hopes were raised and then dashed. *Fraser's Magazine* put the British Government's dilemma over the Cleopatra's Needle in a nutshell when it said 'England appears, from her apparent bewilderment about the matter, to be in the position of the elderly lady who won an elephant in a lottery.'[8] What was to become of the obelisk? This question was posed in 1859 in an article published in the first volume of Charles Dickens' magazine *All the Year Round.*

The last time the writer saw it (not very long ago) a Briton was sitting upon it, knocking off enough of the inscribed stone for himself and fellow travellers with a hammer. The writer expostulated with his fellow Briton, and reminded him that that wonderful relic of bygone days did not belong to him, but had been handsomely presented to the British nation, and therefore belonged to it. "Well, I know it does," he answered, "and as one of the British nation I mean to have my share." ... Is it ever the intention of the British government to bring to England Cleopatra's Needle? If it be not, surely the suggestion of an American merchant, either that it be given to some other nation, or offered to some first-class showman, ought to be adopted. Why waste it, or worse than waste it? Why suffer it to lie there and be broken to pieces, and bit by bit carried off to adorn the mantlepieces or drawing-room tables of travellers who are brutal enough and vulgar enough to hammer at it?[9]

It was just as well that the bulk of the needle lay buried in the sand, for this not only protected it from erosion, but also from the hands of certain other Britons, who when not souvenir hunting had equally bad habits. Another major attraction in Alexandria was Pompey's Pillar, a red granite column erected by the Romans, and British tourists had mutilated its base by scratching their names on it. Obviously vandalism is not a new problem. The intrepid Victorian canoeist 'Rob Roy' Macgregor, who held the honorary position of Captain of the Royal Canoe Club, visited the needle twice, while paddling his way around the Middle East. He published an account of his travels, and described how in 1849 'I found this neglected gift only half buried,' but twenty years later 'it was so completely hidden that not even the owner of the workshop where it lies could point out to me the exact spot of its sandy grave!'[10]

In 1867 the Egyptian Government sold the ground on which the prostrate needle lay to a Greek merchant called Giovanni Demetrio. The new owner intended developing the land, but could not build upon it as the obelisk was in his way. He therefore approached the Egyptian Government and asked them to remove the needle, and as a result the ruler of Egypt, Khedive Ismail Pasha, personally appealed to Britain to come and collect it, but his plea fell on deaf ears. Annoyed at the delay, Demetrio now insisted that the Egyptian Government must remove the obelisk; a demand that was ignored. Unable to evict his unwelcome tenant an angry and distraught Demetrio threatened to break the obelisk up and use the stone as building material. And so it seemed that the fate of the fallen Cleopatra's Needle was sealed, for there it lay helpless, incapable of protecting itself, merely a huge stone which was an embarrassment to Britain, unwanted by the Egyptians, and an obstacle to Demetrio's plans.

2

Some talk of Alexander...

In 1867, in the obelisk's hour of peril, a champion entered the lists resolutely determined to rescue the Cleopatra's Needle from such an ignoble fate, and so to save his country's honour. His name was General Sir James Alexander. During his long military career Alexander had served Britain in a variety of roles. His active service included command of a regiment at the siege of Sebastopol in the Crimean War, while in more peaceful times he had ably completed several tours of duty in diplomatic posts, as well as holding an appointment as senior officer in Canada. He also led several surveying expeditions, and on his return from a particularly successful exploration of Central Africa the tall Scot was knighted in 1838 by his tiny monarch—the nineteen year old Queen Victoria. In September 1867 Alexander visited Paris to attend the International Exhibition, and when crossing the Place de la Concorde the Luxor Obelisk caught his eye. Alexander was captivated by its splendour, and his thoughts turned to the Cleopatra's Needle, and to his grand-uncle Major Bryce who had been closely involved in the abortive first attempt to bring the obelisk to Britain in 1801 as a memorial to the British victories over the French. Later in a discussion with another Briton, Alexander was appalled to learn that the owner of the land on which the needle laid had recently threatened to break the obelisk up if it was not removed. Outraged by this threat of vandalism General Alexander reacted strongly.

I now determined to endeavour to save the national disgrace of the loss and destruction of the trophy—the prostrate obelisk, and I resolved to do my utmost to have it transported to London, to grace the metropolis with a monument similar to those in Rome, Paris, and Constantinople.[1]

On his return to Britain the general sounded out various influential people on the prospect of rescuing the Cleopatra's Needle from the fate awaiting her. Most of those he talked to thought it a highly laudable project, but at the same time were reluctant to provide positive help. For instance, the Keeper of Antiquities at the British Museum favoured the idea but did not feel able to lend his support to any application for a government grant of money to implement it. So, off his own bat, Alexander contacted the Foreign Office, and after due consideration Lord Stanley replied that although Parliament could be asked to vote a sum of money, they were unlikely to do so. Undeterred the general then obtained an introduction to the Chancellor of the Exchequer, Robert Lowe.

I was received very cordially, and asked to produce plans and estimates. In conjunction with Mr Gamgee, of the City of London, Mr. Hill, and Mr. Eassie, C.E., a scheme was prepared with great care for the removal of the obelisk, but the expense was estimated at £15,000, and this induced Mr. Lowe to postpone the undertaking to a more fitting season.[2]

14 General Sir James Alexander, (1803-85). A distinguished army officer who for ten years campaigned vigorously to have the prostrate Cleopatra's Needle brought to Britain.(*The Graphic,* 1878).

With government help obviously out of the question, for the time being at least, a determined General Alexander changed his tactics, and resorted to arousing public interest. During the next few years he propositioned people, wrote countless letters, and lectured to various bodies including the Royal Society of Edinburgh and the British Association. In December 1872 a revised scheme which he had drawn up with the help of Mr Duncan, the Chief Engineer of the Clyde Navigation, was published in *The Engineer*. Briefly, the plan entailed excavating the sand from around the needle and enclosing it in a carriage. This was then to be moved on rails down the foreshore and rolled into the hold of a waiting ship specifically designed for the purpose with a removable bow. Momentarily interest was evoked in the technical press, and various alternative suggestions were made as to how the project could be carried out; however, what little curiosity he managed to produce soon lapsed. The only satisfactory outcome was that the Metropolitan Board of Works granted him a site for erecting the obelisk in an ornamental garden on the Thames Embankment.

Alexander persisted in his campaign, so much so that in some quarters he was apparently regarded as a nuisance, for he relates:

I was now told, in order to discourage me, that I was taking much trouble for an object which was not likely to be accomplished, or worth the labour—that the obelisk was mutilated; was partly built over by the sea-wall of the fortifications; and besides, it was not likely the Khedive would allow its removal after so many years.[3]

Early in 1875 General Alexander resolved to go out to Egypt to determine for himself the true condition of the obelisk, and to find out whether or not permission could still be

15 Palace of Abdin, Cairo. Khedive Ismail Pasha's favourite palace. It now houses a museum and government offices.

obtained to remove it. First, through an influential friend, he obtained an interview with the new Foreign Secretary, the Earl of Derby. The Foreign Secretary was sympathetic to the cause, and although his sympathy did not extend as far as persuading his Government to spend any money, he did at least agree to provide Alexander with a letter of introduction to Major-General Stanton, the Consul-General in Cairo, instructing him to arrange a private audience with the Khedive. Alexander decided to travel by the direct route, rail across Europe to Southern Italy, followed by the four day crossing on a P & O steamship from Brindisi to Alexandria. It was not his intention to hurry, and en route he meant to sample the sights and delights of Florence, Rome, Naples, and of course Pompeii. He later wrote how on 'March 2, 1875, I left London, alone, unprovided with public funds, after purchasing some railroad, steamboat, and hotel tickets from the well-known Mr Cook to prevent delays, and facilitate my progress to and from Italy, Egypt, and the Holy Land.'[4]

He arrived at Alexandria aboard the *Hindostan* on March 19, having immensely enjoyed his travels through Italy. Before he disembarked Alexander engaged one of the traveller's guides who had come aboard offering their services, an intelligent dragoman called Mustapha Adler Ali.

The usual terrific row took place on landing—the scramble to secure the baggage and transport it to the Custom House for examination, and backsheesh to those helping. Then established at the hotel in the Great Square, immediately after which I summoned the dragoman to take me to the obelisks by the sea-shore.

I was particularly impressed with the beauty of the upright obelisk—its graceful and tapering form. The strange hieroglyphics on its best faces, that exposed to the sharp sand-borne wind of the desert much defaced. Then the prostrate obelisk, the object of my voyage and travel, where was it? "There," pointing to a long trench, said Mustapha. "I see nothing," I answered. He called an Arab boy, and directed him to clear off the sand with a stone, and soon a portion of the great mass was revealed. No building, as I was told I might expect, was over it. There it lay, where it had fallen, undisturbed . . . I resolved to do my best to rescue it from its degraded position, and hoped to see it set up on a place of honour in England.[5]

His stay in Alexandria was brief, and he pressed on to Cairo where he put up at the Shepheard's Hotel, at the exhorbitant cost of sixteen shillings a day. As soon as he had settled in he called upon Consul-General Stanton, who immediately set about arranging Alexander's audience with the Khedive, Ismail Pasha. While waiting for the great day, the general pleasantly whiled away his time exploring Cairo with a fellow Briton, visiting the pyramids, and with his expert eye watching the Egyptian infantry and cavalry undergoing training—a sight which impressed him.

The 25th of March was the day I was to be presented to the Khedive. The Consul-General called for me in his carriage, and we drove to the Palace of Abdin. General Stanton was in plain clothes, as it was to be a private audience, but to show respect to his Highness I was in general officer's undress uniform, sword and sash.

Mamlukes were on guard, outside and inside, richly dressed Body Guards in crimson and gold. An officer received us, and conducted us to an anteroom, to wait some time, as is the custom in the East, till the great man is ready to receive his visitors.

At length a secretary came and announced that the Khedive was ready to receive us. We found his Highness at the top of the stairs. A pleasant looking man in good condition, wearing the usual red fez on his head, and dressed in dark surcoat and trousers, and white vest. No signs of rank about his person, all perfectly plain. Different from the Shah and the Persian dignitaries, to whom I had been presented, with others, long ago—when attached to the Persian Mission of Sir John Macdonald Kinneir.

The Khedive, who spoke French, showed us the way to a handsome reception room, and bowed at the door for us to enter first. Of course we declined to do so. He then went to an upper corner, and we sat on either side of him on a divan. The Consul-General said that I was a zealous antiquary, and had come from England about the prostrate obelisk at Alexandria, to examine its condition, and ask permission for its removal from his Highness. He replied, "This obelisk was presented to the British nation by my ancestor, Mahomed Ali Pasha [Mehemet Ali] for services rendered to Egypt; it belongs to Britain. I give it up freely. How is it proposed to be removed?" I showed his Highness the plan I had published in *The Engineer,* of the barge, of the obelisk encased in a wooden frame, and moved on trucks for shipment. He seemed satisfied, and then entered into details about the size and weight of the obelisk. After this he made no difficulty, but said, "Take it by all means".[6]

The conversation then turned to other subjects, notably suppression of the slave trade and Colonel Gordon who was then in the Sudan. Before the audience finally concluded the Khedive graciously consented to a request that his Chief of Harbours and Lighthouses, Admiral McKillop Pasha, be allowed to provide what assistance he could.

For the next four weeks Alexander reverted temporarily to the role of tourist and visited the Holy Land. He returned to Alexandria in late April and took up residence at the home of some friends, the Gisbornes. The general's next job was to see the owner of the land on which the obelisk lay, the Greek merchant Giovanni Demetrio, to obtain permission to

16 Khedive Ismail Pasha, (1830-95). This grandson of Mehemet Ali became ruler of Egypt in 1863. After bringing the country to the brink of bankruptcy he was deposed in favour of his son Tewfik in 1879. Ismail Pasha then went into exile and died in Constantinople in 1895.(From *L'Egypt* by G. Ebers).

enter his property. Signor Demetrio was still in the throes of a long protracted law suit against the Egyptian Government over the removal of his unwelcome tenant, the prostrate Cleopatra's Needle, but as yet he had not carried out his threat to dispose of it for building material. Alexander visited him at his home, a delightful house set in a large luxurious garden on the outskirts of Alexandria. On his first visit Demetrio was unwilling to give an outright yes or no to Alexander's request, since he was intent upon obtaining damages from the government, however, he agreed to give it careful consideration. The general was a wily old campaigner, and the next time he called he was accompanied by his host's attractive wife, Mrs Gisborne, and he later recorded that as he had suspected, feminine charm and influence were of service, for Signor Demetrio succumbed and expressed his pleasure in being able to accede to the request.

As the general began to look deeper into the task of removing the obelisk and transporting it to England, news of his mission quickly spread and he soon found himself the centre of local interest. Not surprisingly some of the British residents had their own ideas of how he should tackle the problem, and needless to say some of the proposals were, to say the least, rather hare-brained. Then, one day, Admiral McKillop introduced him to a young English engineer, Waynman Dixon, who had established a reputation for himself as an antiquary. Some years previously while supervising the erection of a bridge across the Nile at Giza, near Cairo, young Dixon had lived for some months in a tomb on Pyramid Hill. What little leisure time he had was spent exploring the Great Pyramid, and bringing his experience and skill as a Civil Engineer to bear he had been instrumental in the making of some important discoveries.

The meeting between the old soldier and the young engineer was to be of crucial importance, for Waynman Dixon had a most ingenious plan for transporting the needle.

The origin of this Cylindrical plan was on this wise. My brother John Dixon C.E. came out to Egypt in October 1872 for the opening of the Ghizeh Bridge near Cairo, which he had just completed (W.D. being the Resident Engineer), and when in Alexandria we went one morning to inspect the site of the fallen Obelisk, and discussed together the possible means of transport. We made inquiries as to the depth of the sea in front of it, and I then suggested to him the idea of enclosing it as it lay in a cylindrical iron pontoon and rolling it into the sea. He left for England the same day, but so eminently practicable did the idea seem to him that on his arrival he wrote to the papers, saying there were no difficulties in the way of its transport, and that it could be set upon the Thames Embankment for £15000. He was now enthusiastic for its accomplishment, and he wrote me to take soundings across the old harbour of Alexandria, but I was unable to do so before my return from the First Cataract [of the Nile] in June of the following year, 1873, when I reported to him and at the same time sent the result of my calculations as to the necessary size of the Cylinder, etc. The subject, however, dropped so far as anything practical was concerned until the spring of 1875, when General Sir James Alexander came out to Egypt to examine the practicability and cost of the transport .... I then explained to him the Cylindrical scheme with its manifold advantages; and to show the condition of the Obelisk and obtain more correct dimensions I employed men to remove the soil from its upper surface, which we together examined on May 5th 1875, the result being that we found the upper surface in a much better condition than we anticipated.... Encouraged by this result I wrote home to my brother, and at the same time drew up for Sir James a detailed report on the Cylinder Scheme, estimating the cost at £10,000.[7]

With the ground now fully prepared in Egypt, General Alexander returned to England. On his arrival he made an appointment to see John Dixon, and the two men discussed the project in detail. By now the press had realised that something was afoot, and it was rumoured that the needle was either cracked or so badly worn as to be not worth the

17 John Dixon CE, (1835-91). Born in Newcastle-upon-Tyne he became an articled pupil of the railway engineer Robert Stephenson. After acting for some years as the manager of an ironworks he went into business on his own as an engineer and contractor. John Dixon constructed the first railway in China, but was mainly noted for bridge and harbour works. In 1878 he undertook the transportation of the prostrate Cleopatra's Needle from Alexandria to London. His notable achievements include the reconstruction of Hammersmith Suspension Bridge in the 1880s.(*The Graphic*, 1878).

trouble of bothering about, so at his brother's suggestion Waynman had the obelisk completely uncovered to check its condition, and to help scotch the rumours he sent home a set of photographs of it. Waynman also carried out extensive soundings to check the depth of water and the nature of the sea bed adjacent to the site, and then reported the findings to his brother.

Seeing now some little hope of the project being carried out, I further proceeded to elaborate my plans and in July 1875 sent home sketch plans and calculations for the construction of the Cylindrical pontoon, and pointed out the desirability of placing the obelisk with its butt end some distance from the front end of the cylinder, and with its centre below the centre of the Cylinder so as to form its own ballast, besides many other details which were eventually carried out almost to the letter.[8]

Completely convinced of the viability of the project John Dixon wrote to the newspapers offering to personally subscribe £500 towards a fund which he urged should be set up to defray the cost of bringing the needle to Britain. Although some members of the public expressed interest in the idea, his pleas for them to express it in financial terms went unheeded. The Egyptian correspondent of *The Times* incorrectly reported that General Alexander was prepared to foot the bill, but this was emphatically denied by the general in a letter published by the newspaper.

While I have already given much time and trouble to the facilitating the removal of this beautiful monument, and am fully prepared to devote much more of my time and trouble to the accomplishment of this object, I am not prepared to bear the expense of it. Nor do I think that any private person, however rich, should be allowed to undertake what seems to me a national duty[9].

Over the years General Alexander had built up a portfolio of different schemes for rescuing the needle including the one he had published in 1872, plus of course the Dixon plan, and an assortment of other proposals. One idea involved lowering the obelisk down a ramp into the sea, then lifting it into a hopper barge, as used in dredging operations, through the trapdoors in the bottom of the vessel. The barge would then have returned to England under its own power, a rather risky operation as these barges are designed to operate in sheltered coastal waters. A scheme put forward by John Walker, Chief Engineer of the Ramleh Railway in Alexandria, entailed transporting the obelisk through the streets of that city on a carriage, and then simply lashing the needle down on the deck of a large cargo ship. John Dixon had already considered, and rejected, a similar idea, since 'We could not have carried it through its narrow and tortuous streets without the expenditure of a fabulous amount of money in straightening the route[10].' Yet another plan involved dredging a channel from the needle out into deep water, a thought that Dixon had also discarded, for the sea bed consisted of only a few feet of sand with solid rock beneath it, and ...

... to dredge the sand in the face of the strong side current was difficult with the rock underneath, and to blast the rock with the sand above it was equally difficult. It would have been a costly process; and then, even if the canal had been made, what was the ship that we were to get into it, in order to carry the obelisk? We were on an exposed coast with a heavy sea. We had a strong set of the current carrying the sand; and we had also the fact that although our obelisk only weighed about 200 tons, as you may readily understand, a vessel able to carry 200 tons in one solid piece, would require to be a big ship. It would require to be peculiarly strengthened, and we should at once get into very great expense[11].

Elated by the success of his mission to Egypt, Alexander approached the British Government again, and after submitting his portfolio waited hopefully. The reply, when it came, was the same as it had always been. There was no money available. Naturally he was very disappointed; in fact he was downright disgusted with the British Government's attitude. Their refusal to provide the means for accepting the gift not only amounted to snubbing the Khedive, but more seriously in his eyes it was a denial of the heroic services rendered to their country by Nelson and Abercromby. Having progressed this far the general was not prepared to surrender, but being a realist he concluded that his only chance of winning the fight was to raise the money privately. He therefore discussed the problem with an ex-Lord Mayor of London, Alderman Cotton, and they decided to combine forces and try to raise the money in the City. Then, by chance, Alexander fortuitously mentioned his intentions in a letter which he wrote on another topic to the eminent surgeon and dermatologist, Professor Erasmus Wilson FRS.

Wilson, a Professor at the Royal College of Surgeons, was well-known as a benefactor of medical charities. On receipt of the letter he arranged a meeting with General Alexander to discuss the affair, and it concluded with his expressing an interest in providing the necessary finance. After the meeting, a by now enthusiastic Wilson turned to a friend, civil engineer Henry Palfrey Stephenson, for advice on the best way of bringing the obelisk to London. Stephenson carefully studied the various proposals collected by General Alexander, and then announced his verdict. It was to be the Dixon plan. Stephenson knew John Dixon's reputation as an engineer, and he had no doubt of Dixon's ability to bring this ingenious plan to fruition. As a result in November 1876 Erasmus Wilson made an appointment to see John Dixon at his London office.

I called upon Mr. Dixon, whom I had never seen before nor heard of, save through Sir James Alexander. Sir James Alexander had left him a few minutes before I entered. I soon found that Mr. Dixon was a Freemason, hence, all formality and ceremony were at once banished. He told me that he had long contemplated bringing the obelisk to England, and hoped some day to do it himself, when he should be rich enough, he said that he and Mr. Fowler had talked over bringing it, but that political reasons had left the matter in abeyance. He then said, I should enclose the monolith in boiler plate, and roll it into the sea, I would then steady the cylinder by means of bilge plates, ballast it, fix a rudder, fix a cabin and spar deck, and then tow her to England. He said, he thought it might be done for £5000 but he would enter into a contract to do it for £7000[12].

Wilson asked for time to consider the proposal, and then at a second meeting, at which John Dixon was bubbling over with enthusiasm to tackle a venture he had so long looked forward to, Wilson told him the 'undertaking is not an easy one; there may be unexpected difficulties, we *must* succeed; you say you can do it for £7,000, will you undertake to set it up safely on the banks of the Thames for £10,000; no cure no pay?'[13] Dixon accepted Wilson's generous offer without hesitation, although he knew the 'no cure, no pay' condition meant that he would be personally liable for all expenditure if he failed to fulfill his side of the contract, even if his failure was due to circumstances beyond his control. In addition if the operation proved more expensive, he would of course have to find the extra money himself. A week later the two men met again, this time in a solicitor's office, where with the assistance of Alexander and Stephenson they thrashed out the terms of the contract. It was signed on 30 January 1877, and under its terms John Dixon would receive his £10,000 if, and only if, he succeeded in erecting the Cleopatra's Needle on the Thames

18 Professor Erasmus Wilson, (1809-84). An eminent surgeon and dermatologist who in 1876 generously offered to defray the expense of bringing the fallen Cleopatra's Needle to Britain.(*The Graphic*, 1878).

Embankment within two years.

Meanwhile General Alexander had not been idle. In January 1877, while the contract was being drawn up, he approached the Metropolitan Board of Works regarding the site on the Victoria Embankment granted to him in 1872. Permission was again given to erect the needle there on condition it did not involve the Board any expense. The cylindrical barge envisaged in the Dixon plan would need to be towed to England, so Alexander, supported by Admiral Sir Erasmus Ommanney, paid two visits to the Admiralty in a vain attempt to persuade their Lordships to allow a returning warship to undertake the tow. The Admiralty's refusal was on the grounds that the safety of the towing vessel would be jeopardised in bad weather.

In 1875 Alexander had verbally received permission from Khedive Ismail Pasha to remove the needle, but as nothing had been put in writing, there now remained the ticklish task of getting the British Government to acknowledge their ownership. The situation was apparently very delicate, since although the original offer of the obelisk made by Mehemet Ali over fifty years earlier had been renewed on several subsequent occasions, Britain had never done anything about it. The gift apparently had neither been refused, nor officially accepted. All the government had ever done, to put it bluntly, was to ignore it, and the official view in London was that the offer had now lapsed. The Foreign Office seem to have been reluctant to take the initiative; perhaps they were too embarrassed to ask the Khedive, now at long last, 'Please can we have our gift?' The diplomats dithered for a month, so an impatient John Dixon cabled his friend John Fowler, who held the position of engineering advisor to the Khedive, and Fowler promptly sorted the matter out. On 14 March the British Consul-General was summoned to the Abdin Palace, and the Khedive not only officially re-presented the Cleopatra's Needle to Britain, but gave him a letter granting John Dixon permission to remove it.

Back in July 1875 Waynman Dixon had drawn up a preliminary design for the cylindrical barge in which the needle was to be cocooned for its voyage to Britain, but now, at the moment when his plans were about to be finalised he was unfortunately unavailable, having left Egypt the previous November on an expedition to Somalia. So his brother turned again to John Fowler for help, and Fowler rose to the occasion, by giving

35

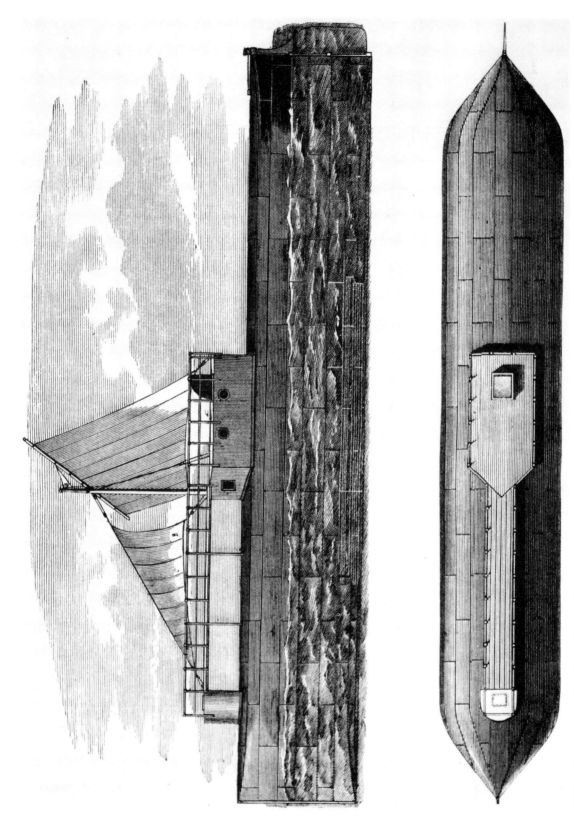

19 The *Cleopatra*. An elevation and plan of this strange cylindrical craft. She measured ninety-two feet long by fifteen feet diameter, and fully laden displaced about 300 tons. (*Engineering*, 1877).

permission for Benjamin Baker, a junior partner in his firm of consulting engineers, to lend a hand. Benjamin (later Sir Benjamin) Baker was a talented young engineer who achieved fame as the engineer of the Forth Bridge and who later reached the top of his Profession when in 1895 he was elected President of the Institution of Civil Engineers. In a technical paper published in 1880 Baker described how he tackled this important commission:

The first thing to be settled was the size of the ship. Widely differing dimensions had been published of the fallen Needle, but on laying it bare and taking exact cross sections [a task performed by Waynman Dixon in 1875], the probable weight was estimated at 186 tons. Adding to this the weight of the ship, 70 tons, that of the stores and ballast, say 34 tons, and allowing a surplus buoyancy of 40 per cent, which is in excess of the usual margin, the given dimensions of 92 feet long, inclusive of the wedge-shaped ends, by 15 feet diameter were arrived at. The vessel had collision bulkheads at the bow and the stern, and seven intermediate watertight bulkheads, through six of which the Needle passed and was wedged thereto by a species of "spring beam" wooden packing, of such strength, or rather weakness, as to break under a considerably less blow than could by any chance injure the Needle.[14]

The cylinder was to be constructed from wrought iron, and on top of it Baker positioned two tiny central cabins surmounted by a steering deck, from which a catwalk or hurricane deck stretched forward nearly as far as the bow. The catwalk terminated in a small turret which 'served the double purpose of splitting the waves and throwing them off the back of the cylinder, and of affording an independent access to the interior of the vessel in the highly improbable event of the strong iron cabin being carried away by a heavy sea.'[15] The vessel was to be assembled around the obelisk from prefabricated parts, and in the middle of March 1877 a contract for these was signed with the Thames Iron Works. The job was speedily executed under the supervision of their naval architect Mr Mackison, for by the first week of June all sixty tons of ironwork had been shipped out to Egypt and lay on the site at Alexandria awaiting assembly.

3

. . . and some of Engineers

That traditional patriotic song *The British Grenadiers* opens with the words 'Some talk of Alexander, and some of Hercules.' In this tale the mantle of Hercules rested upon the shoulders of a handful of engineers who were destined to perform the herculean labours of lifting the prostrate Cleopatra's Needle out of the sands of Egypt, cocooning it in an iron case for shipping to Britain, and re-erecting it in London. Under John Dixon's guidance these tasks were carried out by his fellow engineers Waynman Dixon, Benjamin Baker, and George Double, aided by Henry Carter, an experienced P & O captain.

The Alexandrian end of the operation was entrusted by John Dixon to his younger brother Waynman, who had proved his salt on many previous occasions by supervising the construction of bridges and harbour works in Egypt. However, in April 1877 Waynman had still not returned from his expedition to Somalia, so arrangements were made for the work to be started in his absence. Before even the first spadeful of sand could be removed from around the fallen obelisk, a snag arose in the form of Giovanni Demetrio, the Greek merchant on whose land it lay buried. For ten years Demetrio had wanted to build upon his property, but the presence of the needle had thwarted him. The Egyptian Government had consistently ignored his requests that they should remove the needle, and eventually an irate Demetrio had started legal proceedings against them for damages. After a long drawn out and expensive court action he had recently lost his case; the Egyptian Government having disclaimed any responsibility for the needle. Years before Demetrio had threatened to break it up and use the stone as building material, and most other businessmen would probably have now carried out their threat. But Demetrio was also a keen amateur archaeologist, and as such the thought of destroying an important relic of an ancient civilisation was abhorrent to him. So the obelisk had remained, safe, but unwanted. Then, suddenly, one day in April 1877, workmen arrived out of the blue with the blessing of the Khedive to remove his unwelcome guest. Perhaps Demetrio should have been pleased, but far from it. It galled him that at one moment the Egyptian Government could calmly disclaim any responsibility for the obelisk, and yet the next, without even bothering to consult him, should give it away and grant permission for its removal. Greatly angered at the way he had been completely ignored he erected a strong fence around his Cleopatra's Needle and prevented anyone from trespassing on his land.

When the news of this setback reached John Dixon in London, he decided to resort to tact and diplomacy.

For a moment the position of affairs looked rather embarrassing, and delay at the least appeared inevitable pending judicial inquiry and decision. . . . I despatched a prudent and trustworthy member of my own staff to Alexandria armed with full powers to meet the exigencies of the case. He carried also with him the most friendly letters from Professor Owen, Dr. Birch [of the British Museum], myself and others to M. Demetrio.[1]

The man chosen for this delicate mission was Captain Henry Carter, whose tact and courteous manner were beyond reproach for he had over twenty years service to his credit on the passenger steamships of the P & O. Carter travelled overland across Europe, and in Italy he had a rather strange experience.

Not being able to get accommodation at an inn in a small town, he took up his quarters for the night at a shop where there was a tame goat. He stretched himself on a bench to sleep, and found something nibbling at his feet; he took off his boots and threw them into a corner. In the morning he found that the goat had made mince-meat of them, ate them, and the captain was barefooted. He managed to get a pair of wooden sabots, and clamped about in them till he was able to provide himself with shoes to continue his journey.[2]

On his arrival in Egypt Carter first of all went to Cairo to consult with Mr Crespigny Vivian, the British Consul-General, and then returned to Alexandria and attempted to mollify Signor Demetrio. The letters from leading British archaeologists and antiquaries, with their glowing tributes, eased somewhat Demetrio's ruffled feelings, but he still felt greatly offended at the shabby treatment doled out to him by the Egyptian Government. So Carter went back to Cairo and Mr Vivian personally put the facts of the case to the Khedive, with the result that an official letter, both polite and apologetic, was sent to the aggrieved Greek. The outcome was a change of heart by Demetrio, and on 11 May he wrote to John Dixon telling him

I can have but one thought—that of at once acceding to your request and allowing you to remove the obelisk at present resting on my property. . . . My sole object is to assist you in carrying out the artistic work you have undertaken, assistance which I owe you as a student of archaeology, and as a Greek subject who cannot forget the debt of gratitude which his country owes to the English nation. I have therefore, the honour to inform you that from the present moment the obelisk is entirely at your disposal, and that I waive claim against the Egyptian Government in respect of it.[3]

20 Moving the prostrate needle. Labourers jacking the needle around to bring it parallel to the sea wall at Alexandria.(*The Graphic,* 1878).

Demetrio was as good as his word, and it is on record that henceforth he not only did everything in his power to facilitate the removal of the obelisk, but did so regardless of expense.

The way was now finally clear for work to begin, and Waynman Dixon arrived back in Alexandria in time to take overall charge. His first job was to unearth the obelisk completely, and then to swing it around horizontally until it lay parallel with the sea wall. This was accomplished early in June by lifting the pointed end of the needle out of its trench using a hydraulic jack, and then pushing it into position with a large screw jack. The whole obelisk was next lifted bodily off the ground by four hydraulic jacks, each capable of lifting 100 tons, then gently lowered back down onto a bed of pine logs and sleepers which were to provide a firm working platform. During the swinging operation the ground suddenly gave way, and the needle began to tilt as its moving end started sinking. At Dixon's command Arab workmen quickly shoved timber baulks under the obelisk, nearer the centre, and once the needle had been secured everyone crowded around the hole which had unexpectedly appeared in the ground. Exposed to view was an underground vault containing two human skulls, an incomplete assortment of bones all jumbled up together, and some sealed jars. When these were opened all that was found was a little powdery dust, for the contents had completely mouldered away. Some of those present speculated that this was the tomb of Antony and Cleopatra, but the idea was dismissed as being absurd by those more knowledgeable, for although grave robbers had obviously been there before them the vault itself was by no means grand enough.

While the work of uncovering the prostrate needle had been going on, an archaeological dig was being carried out nearby. When Waynman Dixon examined the fallen needle in 1875 he had noticed four square holes cut in the base, one near each corner. At first he was puzzled about their significance, then it dawned upon him that the Romans might have mounted the obelisk on four metal supports, instead of following the Egyptian custom of resting it directly on the pedestal. Shortly afterwards, while visiting Madrid, John Dixon saw two model obelisks in a museum. These were reputed to have been brought from Pompeii, and both were mounted on four bronze supports. So the mystery of the holes was apparently solved, but to make sure, in May 1877 Waynman obtained permission to excavate around the base of the standing Cleopatra's Needle. Five feet down in the sand he uncovered the top of its granite pedestal, and after he had removed some rough stones from around one corner of the obelisk, there before his eyes lay a bronze support cast in the shape of a large crab. Further careful excavation revealed that metal thieves had been busy at some time in the past, for two of the crabs were missing and most of the legs and claws had been chiselled off the remaining pair. The equilibrium of the obelisk was only maintained by some large stones wedged into position, but even so it was leaning twelve inches out of true. That the crabs had originally done all the work of supporting the needle was beyond doubt, for eight inches of daylight could be clearly seen between the bottom of the obelisk and the top of the pedestal.

A close friend of Giovanni Demetrio, a local physician called Dr Nerutsas-Bey, had followed the dig with great interest, and thanks to his sharp eyesight a most important discovery was made. He thought he detected the faint outline of some Greek characters on the crab, and a thorough cleaning revealed not only a Greek inscription but a corresponding Latin one as well. Tradition had it that the two obelisks had been moved to Alexandria from Heliopolis on the orders of Queen Cleopatra, hence their nickname, but

21 Excavating the base of the upright needle. Waynman Dixon (seen on the right) carried out the excavation in May 1877 and proved conclusively that the Romans had used four large bronze castings to support the obelisk. More importantly inscriptions were found dating the re-erection of the two obelisks at Alexandria as 13BC.(*The Graphic,* 1877)

22 Assembling the cylinder. Positioning the first few watertight bulkheads at Alexandria in June 1877.

now the evidence lay before them. The inscriptions recorded the re-erection of the needles in the eighteenth year of Caesar Augustus (around 13BC), seventeen years after the death of Antony's bewitching lover. Unfortunately due to the difficulty of reading the inscriptions with the crab in situ, the date was misread, the first number in the Roman eighteen being missed. Hence an error of ten years occurred in dating their erection at Alexandria, but this was rectified a few years later when a closer inspection of the crab became possible. Perhaps the two obelisks were brought to Alexandria at Cleopatra's command, and a delay occurred in erecting them, but no one really knows. The prostrate needle fell to the ground several centuries before Waynman Dixon came on the scene, and whether the fall was caused by an earthquake, or by the greed of metal thieves is open to conjecture.

The time had now come to build the cylindrical barge around the needle. After clearing a space beneath part of it one of the watertight bulkheads was assembled in position; then another, and so on. Gradually under the watchful eye of Captain Carter the cylindrical hull of his vessel took shape as one by one the iron plates forming its outer skin were riveted into place. Finally when the tapering bow and stern sections had been added to the main cylinder the Cleopatra's Needle was once again hidden from view, firmly encased in its iron coffin with its butt end facing forward. This phase of the operation had taken two months to complete, having been interrupted for some time in early July by gales.

Meanwhile the portion of the old quay wall in front of the huge iron tube had been

23 The half-way mark in assembling the cylinder. The frames and bulkheads are in position and many of the iron plates forming the outer skin have been riveted in place. Waynman Dixon, complete with furled umbrella, stands at the needle's pyramidion directing operations. (*The Graphic*, 1878).

removed, and gangs of Arab and Maltese workmen wielding spades and pickaxes had shifted several thousand cubic yards of sand and rubble to provide a smooth sloping pathway across the gently shelving beach to the waiting sea. The beach itself and the sea bed had been littered with stone blocks, remnants of the temple whose entrance the two Cleopatra's Needles had once proudly guarded. Some of the stones weighed over twenty tons, and to remove these, and the foundations of a massive wall lying submerged in the shallows, the divers employed to clear the sea bed had to resort to blasting with dynamite. During these clearing operations an assortment of artefacts was found including some unbroken amphorae.

There was also found a portion of circular pavement of Roman workmanship, but as the requirements of the excavators only needed ten yards of this to be uncovered, they were left in the dark as to its original purpose; but apparently it was a pavement surrounding a fountain, and was doubtless in front of the palace, and midway between the two obelisks as they originally stood. Lying on the pavement was a very curious stone image, measuring about twenty inches in length and with large cat's ears. It was carved from a very hard and brittle stone, unlike any other stone there. This was brought back to England, and is now in the possession of a young lady, who sets a high value on it as a rare specimen of a *petrified baby mummy!*[4]

Not surprisingly the site proved a popular local attraction, and each day brought its ever changing crowd of spectators, who would stop for a while to watch the work in

24 Launching the completed cylinder. All the plates have now been riveted in place and the tapering bow and stern sections have been added. Two timber tyres have been fitted to protect the cylinder when it is rolled down the beach.

progress, before continuing on their way. Among the regulars was the Khedive's aunt, Princess Said, who on one of her visits was reported as having halted 'her cortege of soldiers, syces [grooms], and eunuchs, leant forward and watched the operations for a long time, with very genuine expressions of interest,'[5] before resuming her carriage ride. Mr Vivian also always made a point of calling whenever he was in Alexandria.

To help provide stability at sea, the centre of the needle lay four inches below the centre of the cylindrical pontoon. However, to enable it to roll freely down the beach and into its natural element, it was necessary to overcome this imbalance and make the two centres coincide. This was achieved by strapping twelve tons of iron rails as a counterbalance into the recess on top of the cylinder where the cabin was ultimately to be mounted. It was also thought prudent to protect the iron plating of the cylinder from damage while rolling it down to the sea, so a twelve foot length near each end was covered with timber planks six inches thick to form two wide tyres on which the monster could roll, turning it temporarily into what Benjamin Baker described as 'a gigantic 270 ton road-roller'.[6] The timber was firmly clamped in place by large flat iron bands. Offshore two lighters had been securely, or so it was thought, fastened to the sea bed by strong sea anchors. A quarter mile long steel cable, which had generously been provided free of charge by its manufacturer, Newall's of Gateshead, to tow the barge to England, was wrapped nine times around the cylinder, and its free ends were fastened to two crab winches, one on each lighter. The intention was to haul the cylinder down the beach by reeling the cable in on the winches. To control its descent hawsers led inland from the iron casing to provide a braking action in an emergency.

Mr and Mrs John Dixon and Benjamin Baker travelled out from England to witness the launching which was scheduled for 28 August. The day dawned to find everything shrouded in thick mist, an unusual occurrence at that time of year, but almost as though it had suddenly realised it was in the wrong place, the mist evaporated. Anchored close in to the beach were two tugs patiently waiting to be called upon to tow the cylinder around to Alexandria's dockyard, and aboard one of them the three visitors had a front row seat of the proceedings. Wisely John Dixon had decided against holding an official ceremony, since he knew there were so many things which might go wrong in a venture as novel as this. Nevertheless thousands of people were to form a colourful backcloth to his view of the iron cylinder throughout the day. Among those present were representatives of the world's press, including a special correspondent from *The Standard* who sent a detailed report back to London:

Before six o'clock in the morning the winches on board the lighters were at work taking in the slack of the hawsers, whilst on the land side four powerful screw-jacks were being plied against the cylinder. A few yards to seaward two steam tugs were anchored, also ready to lend assistance if required. In a few minutes the huge mass of iron began to roll towards the sea, but so gradually that the movement was all but imperceptible. Hour after hour was thus spent, the cylinder lessening little by little the space between it and the water, till at noon it had made one entire revolution, equal to about 50ft. Notwithstanding the sun, which sent the mercury in the thermometer up to 90 degrees in the shade, the work went on uninterruptedly throughout the day and excited much interest, not only among the European population, but also amongst the Arabs, who crowded every spot from which a view of the operations was obtainable. Working the hawsers from the lighters had soon to be abandoned, as experience showed that, owing to the bad holding ground, the anchors of the latter invariably came home when any great strain was thrown upon them, and the hawsers instead were led to the two tugs which, steaming full speed ahead, communicated to the obelisk just sufficient impetus to keep it in motion. At 5.30pm the iron monster had been laboriously brought to the water's edge, where the wooden launching ways terminated, and a comparatively steep decline commenced. Here the cylinder went off with something like a rush, and took the water with a run of about 12ft., amidst the shouts of the bystanders. After this its progress was as gradual as before, and the screw-jacks had to be kept in constant operation till shortly before 7pm., when it again made a sudden half turn, and rested for the night in 3ft of water.[7]

The work was resumed early next morning as soon as there was sufficient daylight. As before the giant tube showed great reluctance about moving and little headway was made until shortly before noon when it made another sudden rush, but then just as suddenly it abruptly stopped again in seven feet of water—two feet less than the depth Baker had estimated as being necessary to float it. The two tugs strove valiantly all day, repeatedly backing towards the shore to get some slack in the cable, and then running full steam ahead to try and jerk the cylinder into motion. But it obstinately refused to budge, and at sunset the attempt was abandoned. That night the engineers met to discuss the situation, and the following morning, 30 August, Waynman Dixon rowed out to the cylinder to inspect it.

25 The cased obelisk now rests at the top of the launching ways. Two cables lead inland to winches in order to provide a braking action in an emergency.(*Engineering*, 1878).

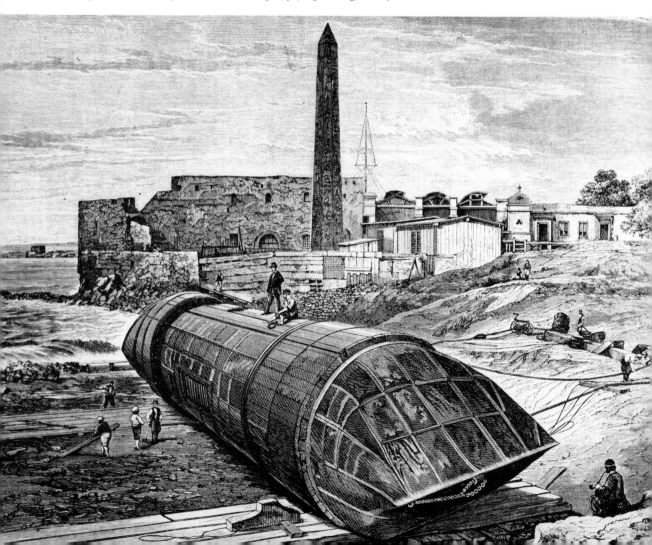

26 Launching the cylinder, 29 August 1877. Overnight the giant tube had rested in three feet of water.

When the man-hole in the deck was opened he discovered to his horror that the tubular shell was half full of water. The only thing to do was to call for pumps and hope for the best.

Soon huge streams of water were seen pouring from the 15in. double barrel pump set going, and it was hoped that the cylinder would soon be cleared. When, however, after three relays of sixteen men each had been at work [manning the hand operated pump], and it was found that the water was in no way reduced, it was evident that there was a serious hole somewhere. A regular diver, in proper diving dress, was then sent down, and from his report it appears a stone hidden in the sand had penetrated the bottom near one of the ends of the cylinder, and so caused the mischief.[8]

The stone in question was a squared building block weighing some twelve hundredweight, and it had made a hole eighteen inches long in the external plating of the cylinder. The Dixon brothers, Baker and Captain Carter held a conference ashore, and there were no doubt some red faces. Three very experienced engineers and a captain of many years standing had all been present, and every step of the operation had been carefully planned. As John Dixon put it 'We had provided bulkheads, we had provided watertight doors through them, and we had so carefully managed that the man whose duty it was to close these doors had forgotten to do so, and all were left open. There is nothing like confession.'[9] If the doors had been closed, only one of the watertight compartments would have been affected, but instead the cylinder was flooded from end to end, more than doubling its weight, and worst of all it was solidly wedged in position by a huge stone block. No wonder the tugs could not shift her. The question was, what should they do next?

A difference of opinion as to the next steps to be taken here occurred between the "home detachment", Mr. J. Dixon and Mr. B. Baker on the one hand and the resident engineer and his staff on the other, and as Mr. Dixon generously refrained from interfering too peremptorily with those who had hitherto ably carried out his plans, some two or three days were lost in attempts to pump dry a vessel which was known to have filled in a few minutes.[10]

Having given his young brother sufficient time to try to solve the problem, John Dixon now decided to take charge. He ordered the construction of a heavy wooden crib, an open-topped box, with a base nine feet square. This was sunk on the seaward side of the cylinder and then filled to the top with iron rails, stones and sand to anchor it firmly in place. A powerful jack was then positioned between the crib and the reluctant cylinder, and eventually the waterlogged monster had been rolled back far enough for the damaged plate to emerge from the water just before noon on 5 September. It was then a simple matter to patch the plate and pump the cylinder dry.

On the 7th the movement of the cylinder recommenced, the tugs steamed ahead, and bit by bit moved into deeper water, the work becoming easier as the mass approached the depth of 9ft., at which it was estimated to float. Shortly before eleven in the forenoon the final move was made, when the cylinder after making a portion of a turn more rapidly than before, was observed to rise and fall with the swell coming in from the Mediterranean, showing unmistakeably that it was at last afloat.[11]

The steel cable and the various restraining hawsers were disconnected, and the two wooden tyres were stripped off. When the iron rails which had been used to counteract the offset weight of the needle were removed, the cylinder, which had been lying heeled over

27 Launching the cylinder. The next day the cylinder stuck and was completely immovable in seven feet of water. A giant stone hidden in the sandy sea bed had pierced the casing. The cylinder was not only flooded from end to end, more than doubling its weight, but worst of all it was solidly wedged in position by the stone. Reproduced from a watercolour painted by John Dixon.

28 The start of the voyage to Alexandria. The tugs *Champion* and *Adjimeh* escorting the cylindrical vessel around to Alexandria Dockyard.

on its side, needed no persuasion to roll into an upright position. One end of the steel cable was now attached to the stern of Messrs Greenfield's tug *Champion,* and the other to the bow of the cylindrical vessel, while the *Adjimeh,* belonging to the Egyptian Government, was coupled up astern by another cable. All was now ready to tow the iron barge around the headland to the Alexandria Dockyard, and late on the afternoon of 8 September the little procession cautiously got under way to the cheers of a large crowd of bystanders.

On the day of passage the sea was high for the time of year, and thick waves, impelled by the northerly wind, rolled on parallel to the break-water, sending columns of spray high into the air. The two tugs in charge of the Needle rolled continuously sponsons under, making it impossible to stand on the bridge without clinging to the rail, whilst the Needle ship came along grandly after them with some forty or fifty Arabs and Maltese sitting unconcernedly on the plain cylindrical top with nothing to save them if the ship made a roll—which she never once did.... Although she behaves exactly as theory indicates, and as was predicted by the engineer, it nevertheless struck everyone with the sensation of a surprise to see the two powerful tugs tossing violently with their floats fanning the air at every roll whilst the little cylindrical ship just let the rollers pass under her without answering to them in the slightest degree, merely bringing her forward and occasionally into the waves and charging the water right and left off her arched back.... It was no easy task to tow her under these circumstances round the breakwater, and after sunset through the dangerous Boghos Pass into Alexandria harbour, and the management of Messrs. Greenfield's tug by her commander was beyond praise. The rudderless cylinder would appear first on one side and then on the other, and again apparently prepared to charge savagely into the broadside of the tug, so that the skipper generally had his wheels going opposite ways, either to coax along the needle or to get out of her way when she charged. Captain Clark was busier perhaps than he had ever been before in towing a craft, but the Arab pilot of course sat cross-legged on the paddle-box smoking cigarettes and looking dreamily ahead as if he had done nothing since his childhood than sit in a tug and tow "Needles" round to Alexandria harbour.[12]

Once the cylinder was safely dry-docked Admiral McKillop generously put the full facilities of the dockyard at the disposal of Captain Carter, who, with the assistance of Waynman Dixon, was to supervise the completion of his command. The temporary patch and damaged plate were removed and a proper repair effected, and two bilge keels, each forty feet long, were securely riveted to the bottom of the cylinder to restrict any tendency she might have to roll in a gale. The cabin, steering deck and hurricane deck were added, the mast was stepped, and the rudder hung on its sternpost. Ten days after entering the dockyard the now completed vessel once again took to the water. On the morning of Wednesday 19 September she was christened *Cleopatra* in a ceremony conducted by Mr Vivian. Originally the Khedive had expressed his willingness to officiate, but unfortunately due to the delay in getting the cylinder afloat he was unable to attend, having returned to Cairo, so the British Consul-General stepped into the breach. The guests included Princess Said, Giovanni Demetrio, representatives of the Egyptian Government, foreign diplomats, and some of the more prominent members of the British community. The actual christening was performed by the daughter of Admiral McKillop in the traditional manner by breaking a bottle of champagne, but on the stern of the vessel

29 *Cleopatra* afloat in the dry-dock. The now completed vessel gaily decked out for the christening ceremony, which was held on Wednesday 19 September 1877.(*Strand Magazine, 1899*).

instead of her bow. The 150 guests then attended a special luncheon where a jubilant John Dixon and his wife acted as hosts.

Captain Carter had engaged a boatswain who was to receive £50 for the voyage to England, and for his crew signed on six Maltese: five seamen at £20 a head, plus a carpenter at £25. These rates were well above the average for a voyage anticipated to take four weeks, and are a reflection of the average seaman's wariness about accepting a berth on such a strange looking craft. A British merchant ship, the *Olga,* was due to sail from Alexandria with a cargo of grain for Newcastle-upon-Tyne, and Carter made arrangements for her to tow the *Cleopatra* as far as Falmouth. A tug would then take over for the final leg of the journey up the English Channel and into the Thames. Initially Captain Booth of the *Olga* asked £1,000 for the towing operation, then after some discussion a bargain was struck between the two captains for £900, half payable in advance, and the remainder on completion of the tow. The *Olga* was an iron-hulled screw steamer displacing 1,330 tons fully laden built at Sunderland in 1870. She was powered by a 130hp steam engine and the length of the vessel was 251 feet. Her owners were the St Andrew's Steam Company of Liverpool.

As has already been mentioned the axis of the needle lay below the centre of the *Cleopatra's* cylindrical hull to help make the barge stable at sea. In the dockyard twenty tons of iron rails were laid between the frames at the bottom of the vessel in order to further lower its centre of gravity and hence improve stability. She then floated with nearly two thirds of her cylindrical hull immersed, the draught being nearly ten feet. The iron ballast was merely held in place by a wooden floor consisting of planking one inch thick—a fact which all concerned would soon have cause to regret bitterly.

4

The *Cleopatra*

Friday 21 September dawned full of promise with a light airy breeze and calm seas. As the sun climbed steadily on its way up the clear blue sky spectators began to flock to the Alexandria Harbour, and by the hour appointed for the departure a large crowd, including most of the local British community, were there to wish the *Cleopatra* bon voyage. Captain Booth slowly got the *Olga* under way and as he cautiously started towing his charge towards the harbour entrance cheers rang out from the quayside. Friday was not perhaps the most auspicious day to begin a voyage, and among the crowd watching the departure were a few old salts who looked upon a Friday sail as an ill omen, and their heartfelt best wishes went out to the crews of the two vessels. Before long the little convoy was lost to sight in the shipping in the harbour, and then it was gingerly edging its way out into the Mediterranean. Waynman Dixon was aboard the *Olga*, in case his services were required, but of course, as captain, Carter had sole responsibility for the *Cleopatra*.

For months Captain Carter had been itching to get to sea. During his long spell ashore at Alexandria he had suffered, both from a recurring complaint contracted years before in the Orient, and from the constant anxiety of the launching, docking, and fitting out of his unusual craft. Would she behave as her designers predicted? With her cylindrical shape they were confident she would not roll, and their forecast that the waves would merely slip over her had proved correct in the short tow around the headland to the dockyard for fitting out. Others had said that she must roll because of her circular shape. The question that nagged at the back of Carter's mind was, what would happen when they were out in the open sea with a gale blowing? Now that the waiting was over, he was glad to be at sea again, even though it meant he would soon have the answer to his question. Later Carter was pleased to be able to personally report that the 'little vessel justified in every respect the confidence of her designers, for even in the rough weather experienced...not a drop wetted the steering deck over the cabin.' The *Cleopatra* lay very low in the water and her bow was 'covered by every wave with which it came in contact, but the small turret at the bows supporting the hurricane deck split each wave, and throwing the halves on each side, left the deck-house clear' just as Benjamin Baker had assured him it would. Her only vice was a habit of pitching with unusual violence and rapidity, caused by the unevenly distributed weight of the obelisk, but this was to some extent offset by her complete resistance to rolling since 'the cylindrical form of the hull allowed the sea to slip over it without causing the smallest disturbance.'[1]

Shortly after leaving Alexandria the boatswain was taken ill with what was later diagnosed as inflammation of the liver (possibly caused by a partiality for the bottle), and with his second-in-command laid up Carter had no alternative but to stay on watch all

30 On the voyage. The *Cleopatra* pitching up and down as the *Olga* tows her through some stormy weather.(*The Graphic,* 1877).

night, every night, and to grab what sleep he could during daylight hours. A day later another crew member was also confined to bed, this time due to an injured foot, and this temporarily reduced the number of effective men under Carter's command from seven to five. For the first few days of the voyage the sea remained calm, and the sky was a brilliant blue without a trace of cloud in sight, and it was very hot. At night the men preferred sleeping as best they could on deck, since in the confines of their little cabin the heat was stifling. On the Sunday Carter was heartened to see the off-duty members of his Maltese crew solemnly reading their bibles, and in general observing the sabbath. Good progress was being maintained despite the tendency of the *Cleopatra* to occasionally yaw to one side or the other, and by now everyone was getting acclimatised to her strange pitching motion. Monday brought a change in the weather. The wind began to freshen from the west, and the resulting swell caused the *Cleopatra* to pitch deeper and more frequently—to the discomfort of all on board—and standing on the steering deck was rather like being at the centre of a giant see-saw.

Every six hours, as regular as clockwork, Carter would dive down through a small man-hole in the floor of his cabin in order to examine personally all eight interior compartments of his vessel for signs of a leak, and to check that the wooden packing wedging the obelisk in position was secure. This entailed his crawling in the darkness over, and under, the obelisk, with only a candle to light his way, for there was insufficient room for him to carry a lantern. At each of the seven watertight bulkheads he needed to open a tiny door and squeeze through with the tallow candle held in his mouth. While performing this arduous and unpleasant duty he had what he later laughed off as an amusing experience.

53

31 The cabins of the *Cleopatra*. Captain Carter surveys his tiny domain, while two members of the crew are performing chores in their equally small cabin. (*The Illustrated London News,* 1878).

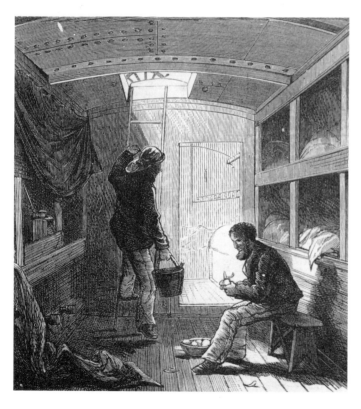

He had got to the end of his beat and was down beneath the obelisk and crawling among the water-casks and great timber beams, when the candle which he carried in his mouth began to burn his nose, so he dropped it down among the iron ballast and was in utter darkness. At the best of times it was no easy matter to get up the circular sides of the ship, and on this occasion it took more than half an hour before he could grope his way back and get into the open air. These man-holes were rather small, and during the first part of the voyage he had some difficulty in squeezing himself through, but after a little experience and, with regular and simple diet, he could slip through like a half-starved rat.[2]

Six days out from Alexandria, on the afternoon on 27 September, having averaged between five and six knots, and with half of the Mediterranean safely behind them, the little flotilla passed about ten miles to the south of Malta. By now the crew were feeling fed up with the strange antics of the *Cleopatra,* and were probably a little homesick as well, for as soon as the familiar shape of Malta loomed over the horizon they begged their captain to put into Valetta. Captain Carter declined, not only because there was no reason to do so, but he feared that given the chance his men would desert. Instead he issued a round of grog, and then later when he was fully satisfied that his crew were now in a happier frame of mind, he retired to his cabin to split a bottle of champagne with the invalided boatswain.

Although the *Olga* and *Cleopatra* were close enough for messages to be passed by speaking trumpet, in stormy weather this method was likely to be unreliable. A signalling system had therefore been devised to enable messages to be quickly and easily passed between the two vessels. In daylight they were chalked on a blackboard which was then held aloft, and at night combinations of different coloured lights could be used as a code for sending pre-arranged signals. One dark and blustery night around ten o'clock the lookout on the *Olga* was startled into action by a distress rocket sent up from the *Cleopatra.* This was immediately followed by signal lights meaning 'Stop—want assistance,' and it was obvious that the tow had parted since the *Cleopatra* was fast dropping astern. As the *Olga* turned back a seaman reported to Captain Booth that the tow-line was still attached to the *Olga,* but was hanging limply at her stern. It took time to haul in the 3½ inch diameter steel rope, and it was midnight before the end came over the *Olga's* taffrail. The rope in fact was intact, but the shackle connecting it to the *Cleopatra* had broken across the eye after being repeatedly strained by her pitching action. In the darkness it would have been too dangerous to attempt to reconnect the tow-line, so the two vessels lay hove-to in close company until first light. Within the hour the repair had been effected, and once more the *Olga* was steaming steadily on her way with the *Cleopatra* following at her heels, albeit a trifle friskily, darting first to the left, then to the right, like an excited puppy, with Carter doing his best to check her antics using the rudder.

As they progressed westwards the weather began to deteriorate rapidly, and soon in the midst of a violent thunder-storm the *Olga* was having to battle her way along the North African coastline against strong headwinds. Partly due to his heavier than expected coal consumption, and partly in an effort to avoid the worst of the storm, for the barometer was still falling, Captain Booth signalled his intention to make an unscheduled stop by putting into Algiers. The crew of the *Olga* were given shore leave, and proceeded to disgrace themselves. They are reported to have all got drunk, and fighting drunk at that. When the Chief Officer tried to round them up for the return to the ship, one of the seamen assaulted him tearing off half of his moustache. Twenty-three hours after putting into Algiers the *Olga* was ready for sea again having replenished her bunkers, and as the weather now had eased, Captain Booth was keen to depart. Carter had refused his crew's pleas for shore leave, but one of them had his wish granted, although not in the way he had intended. As they were putting out to sea the unfortunate Maltese got his leg trapped, and nearly severed, in a coil of hawser. The injured man was landed and sent to hospital.

At Algiers Waynman Dixon had taken the opportunity to write to his brother. In the letter he told him, 'I thought Carter looked careworn; he must have a terribly anxious time, and is constantly on deck, as his boatswain is laid-up ill. . . . He can get no rest, day or night, and I wonder how anyone can sleep in such a "rocking-horse," pitching, almost constantly, fifteen times a minute.'[3] Now, with his small crew further depleted by the accident, Carter well and truly had his hands full. He soon found it necessary to turn his hand to tasks which were not exactly among the normal duties of a captain—but he buckled down to them with a will. Like an ordinary seaman he had to take his spell at the wheel, which no doubt did not ruffle his dignity too much, but he also found himself performing more mundane tasks, such as trimming lamps at night, and even helping to prepare meals. Throughout the voyage Carter never slept at night while at sea, and the only time he took his clothes off was to wash himself and change them. The *Cleopatra* was no P & O steamer, and Captain Carter must have often wished he was back in command of a passenger ship, with its orderly life and creature comforts. On 5 October he made the following entry in his log and from its tone it is obvious the strain was beginning to tell, although as yet he was far from reaching the end of his tether.

This is a most unpleasant night. The swell is high and confused, and the *Olga* seems determined to tow us through the water or under it. I wish she would break down, for the quick pitching motion is almost unbearable. Sixteen pitches per minute—each one sending the water over the hull, fore and aft, and a good deal of spray over all. My bed, the foresail, is saturated, and I walk about in preference to sitting below, where all is close, impure and hot.[4]

However, there were times when the weather, his duties, and the crew, allowed Carter to briefly relax his vigil.

One night the captain, sitting forward, smoking his pipe and watching his charge, two men at the wheel suddenly left it, ran to the captain, called 'Debil!, debil!' and pointed aloft. It was St. Elmo's light at the mast-head, a ball of fire—not unusual in the Mediterranean in stormy weather, and the air full of electricity.[5]

The Maltese were a superstitious bunch, and after the above incident some of them were afraid to go down below into the darkness to assist the captain in his routine inspection. Ever since he had lost the candle, Carter had taken a seaman with him to carry a spare light. We shall never know what hidden terrors the frightened seamen thought might be lurking in the dark belly of that never tiring sea monster as she perpetually dived in and out of the waves. The crew were missing their compatriot sent to hospital at Algiers, and all round their spirits were very low. One thing is certain—they considered the *Cleopatra* to be an unlucky ship. To cheer them up and help keep their minds occupied, Captain Carter issued a large glass of grog to every man, and gave each of them a half hour spell on the hand pump, even though the *Cleopatra* was not making any water worth talking about. However, in spite of all he could do, the crew were unhappy, and there was talk among them of jumping ship at Gibraltar—if they got the chance.

Four days out from Algiers another storm blew up, and as usual the wind was from the

32 The signalling system. Communication between the *Cleopatra* and the towing vessel was effected in daytime by chalking messages on a blackboard. At night pre-arranged signals could be sent using different combinations of coloured lights.(*The Illustrated London News*, 1878).

33 Algiers Harbour.

west impeding their progress, but fortunately the bad weather passed quickly by, and it was fine again long before they caught their first glimpse of the Rock of Gibraltar late on the following morning, Sunday 7 October. Once the two vessels were safely moored in the harbour, Captain Carter and Waynman Dixon went ashore. After posting letters to England, and cabling their safe arrival to John Dixon, the two men looked around for sailors wanting a berth, and engaged an additional two seamen to crew the *Cleopatra*. Meanwhile Booth had been busy organising fresh supplies of victuals and refuelling the *Olga*. Glad of the opportunity Carter had made sure of getting a good night's sleep, and at 1.45pm the next day, in fine weather, the *Olga* resumed her journey home with the *Cleopatra* obediently keeping station astern. Thirty six hours later the light at Cape St Vincent, on the south-west corner of Portugal, could be seen ahead, and just after daybreak they rounded the Cape and turned north. The Atlantic swell now made itself felt, the rollers coming from the north-west, but although the *Olga* started to roll, the *Cleopatra* rode the swell completely unconcerned, bobbing up and down in the water like a duck. The fine weather and light winds persisted as the *Olga* steamed steadily northwards. On 11 October they passed the busy estuary of the River Tagus, where many local craft altered course to get a better view of this unusual procession.

Just before dusk on Saturday 14 October they passed Cape Finisterre on the northern tip of Spain, and entered the Bay of Biscay with the light southerly wind doing what little it could to help them on their way. So far their luck with the weather had held, and if only Dame Fortune would smile upon them for a few more days they would reach the far side of this notorious bay and enter the English Channel. Fate, however, had ordained otherwise, for at daylight the next morning there were unmistakeable signs of an approaching storm, and stormy-petrels and other sea birds were flying about their rigging. Then, just after 8am a vicious squall burst upon them from the SSW, and for half an hour the *Olga* and *Cleopatra* were lashed by torrential rain and hail. Within a few hours the wind had risen to gale force and the sea was running high enough to cause the *Cleopatra* to pitch very deeply. As the day wore on the barometer fell further, the weather deteriorated more and more, and the *Cleopatra* incessantly pitched rapidly and violently up and down, up and down, up and down. . . . The ever strengthening wind was now beginning to veer round towards the west, and at times it brought with it sudden squalls of hurricane force replete with thunder and lightning.

Aboard the *Cleopatra* the crew were huddled in their cabin, except that is for two men unfortunate enough to be on duty. As they manned the wheel and kept a look-out for signals from the *Olga,* the two Maltese stole fearful glances astern to where on her port quarter mountainous waves kept roaring up—as though intent on swallowing the *Cleopatra*—before breaking harmlessly over her. Conscious of the fear in his men's eyes, Carter rigged a screen up out of a hammock, ostensibly to keep the wind and hail off the men, but in reality to prevent them watching the huge waves bearing down upon their tiny craft. Carter later wrote:

So long as the vessel was before the wind I had no cause for anxiety, although the whole of the after part of the vessel was frequently immersed, the sea occasionally rolling over the cabin. The wind, however, began to veer to the westward, and I felt sure it would work round to a furious gale from the N.W. As the sea became quarterly it broke heavily against the deck-house, and I had serious fears of it being swept away. I made up my mind to heave-to, and signal the *Olga* as follows:- "Prepare to heave-to, head to wind." Captain Booth acknowledged my signal, and replied, "Greater risk to tow-line if hove-to."[6]

It was now past four o'clock in the afternoon, and Carter reluctantly decided to hang on for a while longer to see if the weather would improve. Instead it continued to worsen by the minute. The light was already beginning to fade and a very worried Carter urgently signalled to the *Olga* requesting her to heave to. This time Captain Booth responded to his appeal, and with great skill performed the difficult task of bringing the bow of the *Olga* round to head into the wind. The *Cleopatra* tried to follow suit, but as Carter slowly brought her around a tremendous wave struck the vessel completely overwhelming her. If it had not been for the deck-house, the cylindrical hull would probably have shrugged the water off without rolling, but this time the deck-house took the full impact squarely on its port side and the *Cleopatra* was hurled violently over on to her starboard beam ends. As the stricken *Cleopatra* heeled over with Carter hanging grimly on to the rail, he felt something move beneath his feet in the bowels of the ship, and he didn't need to be told what it was.

The timber work used to secure the iron rails employed as ballast gave way, the rails shifted, and the vessel lay over at an angle of more than 45 deg. from the perpendicular. I soon opened the man-hole door in the cabin, and got my crew into the hold to right the ballast. I found the vessel was making a little water at the upper bolt holes; the gale was at its height, and the seas were breaking completely over us. I therefore made signals of distress to the *Olga,* but still kept working at the ballast. In a few hours a great portion of the ballast had been replaced, and the vessel became a little more upright, when a heavier sea than usual threw us over, and the ballast went back to its former position.[7]

Realising how critical their position was, and with many of his crew in a panic, Captain Carter decided they had no alternative but to abandon ship. He accordingly tried to signal his intentions to the *Olga,* but due to the intensity of the gale and the blackness of the night (by now the *Cleopatra's* signalling lights had been washed away), Captain Booth could only make out that they needed assistance, and at first did not realise how serious the position was. The lifeboat of the *Cleopatra* was little more than a rowing boat twelve feet long by four feet wide fitted with cork buoyancy bags, and it was lashed to the port side. Unfortunately this was also the windward side, where it would have been foolhardy indeed to try and board in that tempestuous sea. At Carter's order the lifeboat was lowered into the sea at the end of a rope in an attempt to get it to drift around the stern of the *Cleopatra* and into the shelter of her leeward side. When rounding the stern the rope snagged, and the lifeboat was swept under the rudder yoke by the heavy seas and battered to pieces.

Meanwhile aboard the *Olga* Captain Booth was doing his utmost to assist, however, the storm and the darkness hampered him. 'We slowed engines and got as close as practicable to make out what was wrong; but we were unable to distinguish what was said, signals of distress continuing, and also shouting. The gale taking off a little, we made out "foundering; send a boat." [8] Booth called for volunteers, and Second Mate William Askin stepped forward, to be joined by boatswain James Gardiner and four able seamen. At 9.20pm Booth rang stopped engines, and the six courageous men boarded a boat which had been swung out in readiness on the davits.

We lowered away the boat, got her unhooked and clear of the ship without accident. We saw her close to the *Cleopatra* and anxiously awaited her return. The boat not returning by 11 o'clock, we hailed the *Cleopatra* and asked if the boat was with her. We could not make out the answer, but supposed it was that she was alongside, as the signals of distress ceased.[9]

Sadly nothing could be further from the truth. As Askin and his plucky volunteers approached on the leeward side of the *Cleopatra* a line was thrown to them. At first a seaman managed to grab it, but with the boat being badly buffeted by the waves he lost his grip on the rope. There was no time for a second attempt. As the boat was swept past the *Cleopatra* Askin could be heard exhorting his men to slack away on their oars. But to no avail, for as they passed the stern of the *Cleopatra* and were about to disappear into the darkness, a gigantic wave bore down on them, and after briefly rearing high over their heads engulfed their tiny craft. When the wave had passed the stunned watchers on the deck of the *Cleopatra* could see nothing but the angry seas and the blackness of the night.

With his own lifeboat smashed to smithereens, and the *Olga's* attempt to rescue them having ended in failure, six brave men almost certainly having gone to a watery grave, Carter now knew that if they were lucky enough to survive the night it would be solely through their own efforts. His first thought was to cut away the mast, since the leverage exerted by it was hindering the attempts to right the *Cleopatra*. However, they were only partially successful, for although the mast itself and the port rigging were cut away, they could not reach the rigging on the starboard side. As a result, still attached by some of the ropes, the mast lay alongside in the water, bumping continually against the hull. By midnight, driven on by their captain, the crew had miraculously almost succeeded in relashing the iron rails used as ballast, and the *Cleopatra* was not only nearly upright again, but had been safely brought round head to wind. Suddenly, a much stronger than usual gust of wind caused her to yaw sharply to port, and on being presented with the whole of her starboard side to act upon the wind and the waves had little difficulty in tossing her right over again, this time onto her port beam ends, where she remained at a greater angle than ever before, for inevitably the ballast had once more broken loose. Throughout most of the night Carter urged his weary and dejected men on, and they vainly struggled to fasten the iron rails down. However, no sooner had they managed to secure some of them and the *Cleopatra* had started to right herself, then the wind and the seas contemptuously threw her back. Eventually, one by one the crew abandoned their hopeless struggle, too weary to continue the fight for survival. Some prayed for deliverance, others just lay where they had fallen and waited for the end. All any of them could do now was wait. If fate was kind and they lived to see the dawn, if the gale moderated, if . . .

Aboard the *Olga,* just after midnight, the look-out reported that the *Cleopatra* appeared to have heeled right over to port. Then fresh cries of distress could be faintly heard, and Captain Booth's heart sank for he now feared for the safety of his lifeboat crew.

Hearing cries of "Foundering fast," "Boat adrift," "Send boat to take us on board," and "Haul the line in," we slipped the tow-rope and manoeuvred our ship close to the *Cleopatra;* but the sea was so heavy, and we drifted so much faster than the *Cleopatra,* that we could not hold our position. At 2am we sent a messenger buoy to sweep her with a line, so that the crew might grapple it and be hauled on board by us; but the attempt failed. The wind then was more moderate, but there was a heavy sea running, our ship rolling and pitching very heavily, and shipping much water. There were no volunteers to man another boat, and we had no recourse but to keep close to the *Cleopatra* till daylight. At 5am we slipped another cask as buoy, but again failed. At daylight we got close to the *Cleopatra,* and after several ineffectual attempts to throw a line aboard, we succeeded at 6.30. We then sent a 5in line to keep the vessel in position, we being to leeward, and lowering an unmanned boat, we sent her off with a line, and succeeded in rescuing all hands.[10]

The rescue was by no means an easy affair. The storm had abated, but the swell was still high and dangerous. As the small boat surged up and down alongside the *Cleopatra,* her crew managed with difficulty to jump aboard one by one, except that is for the two invalids. The Maltese with the injured foot and the boatswain, who was still ill, caused complications, but at last it was the turn of Captain Carter to join his eight crew members. Slowly the boat was hauled back to the side of the *Olga,* and soon they were all safely on deck, thankful to be still alive, but minus all their belongings except for the clothes on their backs. It was now 7.40am, and after a quick word with Carter, Captain Booth rightly decided that his first priority was the missing boat and its crew, for although there were unlikely to be any survivors, there was no certainty that they had perished. Booth ordered that the hawser joining the two vessels be cut, and then they steamed off at full speed. Every man who could be spared manned vantage points in the rigging and at the mastheads. Soon a look-out aloft spotted something in the water, but hopes were dashed

34 Rescue. The crew of the *Cleopatra* about to board an unmanned boat sent by the *Olga* just after dawn on Monday 15 October 1877. The engraving is based on a sketch drawn by Captain Carter.(*The Illustrated London News*, 1877).

when it turned out to be the messenger buoy released earlier. Shortly afterwards a boathook was seen, then some oars. For three hours the *Olga* searched fruitlessly along the track which a drifting boat would have taken, but of Askin and his courageous crew there was no trace. Reluctantly Booth abandoned the search and turned back to the position where they had left the *Cleopatra*. They soon found her mast floating forlornly on its own, but of the *Cleopatra* herself there was no sign. After several hours had been spent searching the area, they concluded that she must have foundered, so early in the afternoon Booth put his ship back on course for Falmouth, which they reached two days later on the evening of Wednesday 17 October.

Ashore John Dixon was anxiously awaiting their arrival. Earlier he had been alarmed by a telegraph message reporting that the *Olga* had been sighted off the Lizard—without the *Cleopatra* in tow. When she docked Dixon hurried aboard to be met by his brother Waynman, and thank heavens, Captain Carter. Soon the sorry tale had been told, and Dixon's concern about the needle faded when he heard the distressing news of the lives lost in the vain rescue attempt. Tragically, ashore awaiting the arrival of the *Olga* was a telegram from William Askin's young wife bringing the happy news of the birth of their first child. At John Dixon's suggestion a fund was set up to provide for the dependents of the six men, all of whom came from Liverpool, and to start it off he generously donated £250. In an announcement published a few days later in *The Times* John Dixon appealed to the public to send contributions to the Liverpool agents who acted for the *Olga,* Messrs William Johnston and Company. Later a plaque was erected as a permanent memorial to those brave Liverpudlians.

5

The Proverbial Needle

When the *Olga* docked at Falmouth bearing her sad tidings, John Dixon had naturally been very upset, especially over the deaths of the six brave seamen; yet he could not bring himself to believe that the *Cleopatra* had really sunk. Despite close questioning Captain Carter was adamant that when he had abandoned the *Cleopatra* her seams were watertight, and all her hatches were securely battened down. When the freak wave threw her onto her beam ends the ballast had broken loose and prevented her recovery, but Dixon knew that due to her unusual design it was impossible for the *Cleopatra* to capsize completely. He reasoned that if her hull remained intact she must still be afloat, a view shared by her designer Benjamin Baker. Carter was less confident, and appears to have been trying to put a brave face on things when he said

> I had every confidence in the calculations, and was quite sure the *Cleopatra* would come right side upwards sooner or later: but during the fury of the storm, and with my Maltese crew on their knees praying around me, I couldn't help reflecting that she might be an inconveniently long time in doing it.[1]

Dixon is reported to have consoled him with the words 'Cheer up, Carter, she'll float again, and you shall bring her up the Thames.'[2] So convinced was he that the *Cleopatra* had survived the destructive powers of the hurricane, that the following morning John Dixon contacted the First Lord of the Admiralty and urged him to despatch a fast steamer post-haste, not only in the hope of rescuing the needle, but to remove a potentially dangerous hazard from a busy shipping lane. However, at that very moment news was being received in London by telegraph from Spain that fully justified Dixon's faith in the *Cleopatra*. Lying low in the water she had been as difficult to find in those heavy seas as the proverbial needle, yet within hours of Captain Booth abandoning the search for the *Cleopatra* another ship had steamed down from the north unaware of what lay in her path.

A week earlier, on 9 October, the 197 ton screw steamship *Fitzmaurice* had sailed from Middlesbrough with a cargo of pig iron destined for the port of Valencia on the Mediterranean coast of Spain. The violent storm which had led to the abandonment of the *Cleopatra* wreaked widespread havoc and destruction throughout the British Isles and Western Europe, and was the culmination of many days of gales experienced by the sixteen man crew of the *Fitzmaurice*. The ship struggled against strong headwinds down the English Channel and out into the Bay of Biscay, and then on Sunday 14 October the full fury of the westerly gale struck her. For the best part of twenty-four hours Captain Evans was forced to heave to until the wind and seas had moderated enough to allow him to put his ship back on course at 9am on Monday morning. Late in the afternoon the look-out

THE ILLUSTRATED LONDON NEWS

REGISTERED AT THE GENERAL POST-OFFICE FOR TRANSMISSION ABROAD.

No. 1998.—VOL. LXXI.　　SATURDAY, OCTOBER 27, 1877.　　WITH TWO SUPPLEMENTS} SIXPENCE. By Post, 6½d.

35 Abandoned. The *Cleopatra* lying on her beam ends in the Bay of Biscay on Monday 15 October; left to the mercy of the elements she is repeatedly dipping her bridge deck into the heavy seas.*(The Illustrated London News,* 1877).

reported an object ahead lying low in the water on the port side, so Captain Evans changed course to investigate. At first it appeared to be the bottom of a ship which had capsized, but as they steamed closer, with the aid of his glasses Evans made out the name *Cleopatra*—a name he was familiar with from the press reports of the early part of her voyage. Until that moment he had of course been unaware of her predicament, for Captain Carter and his crew had only been rescued from the *Cleopatra* that very morning.

The *Fitzmaurice* circled the *Cleopatra* at a safe distance but despite hailing her repeatedly there appeared to be no sign of life on board. An attempt at salvage was obviously worthwhile, since in spite of her lying on her beam ends and repeatedly dipping her bridge into the sea as waves struck her—like an ungainly floundering whale—she seemed to be in no imminent danger of sinking. Evans was keen to get a tow-line aboard her and establish salvage rights as soon as possible, and he ordered his second-in-command to prepare a boat. The officer in question objected strenuously for the sea was running dangerously high, and when there were no volunteers to man the boat Evans cancelled the order. By now dusk was falling, and the *Fitzmaurice* spent a difficult night steaming close up to the *Cleopatra* so as not to lose sight of her.

By six the next morning the Chief Officer had a boat ready and waiting. Overnight the weather had improved somewhat, and after exhibiting great reluctance three men—lured by the prospect of their share of the salvage money—volunteered to join the Chief Officer in the boat. As soon as they left the shelter of the side of the *Fitzmaurice* their tiny craft was at the mercy of the heavy seas and gusting wind. After what seemed an age, by straining on their oars they covered the short distance separating the two vessels, and rounded the bow of the *Cleopatra.* Here the four men were confronted by the daunting sight of the heaving bridge, alternately rising in the air above them and then slapping down again into the water. Apart from pitching up and down, and rolling on her port beam ends as she drifted with the wind, the *Cleopatra* was also moving in a weird circular path—like a fairground attraction designed by a madman. The rolling action brought what was left of her rudder into play, the remnants of which were jammed to one side, and each time she rolled the *Cleopatra* also swung, such that every three or four minutes she turned a full circle boxing all the points of the compass. The only chance of boarding her was to leap for the open deck of the bridge when it reached the bottom of its downward swing, for there was nowhere else on that smooth cylindrical hull where a man could hope to gain a safe footing and find a handhold. While two men rowed the other two bravely and foolhardily took it in turns to try to jump aboard that bucking monster. Time and again they failed and ended up in the sea, only to be hauled back on board their little craft by a rope tied around their waist, to lie wet, cold, and gasping, on the boards like an unlucky fish.

Eventually, over one and a half hours after leaving the *Fitzmaurice,* a desperate attempt by the tired Chief Officer was rewarded with success. Amazingly, by noon not only had the remaining portion of the original tow-rope and other wreckage likely to affect the towing operation been cleared away, but two nine inch hawsers had been passed from the *Fitzmaurice* and securely fastened to the *Cleopatra.* All was now ready for towing to begin, and the nearest port was the Spanish naval base at Ferrol some ninety miles to the south on the north-west corner of the Iberian Peninsula.

Two hours of towing in those moderately heavy seas was more than enough for the tow-ropes and they both parted. In reality they were too small to be dignified with the name tow-rope, but they were the best that a cargo ship the size of the *Fitzmaurice* could muster.

66

Fortunately as the day had progressed the heavy seas had been subsiding, so although the task of getting a line aboard the *Cleopatra* had to begin again, this time at least it proved to be an easier and far less dangerous affair. Towing was now carried out at a lower speed to reduce the strain on the ropes. The following morning, Wednesday 17 October, the wind veered to the south-east and as it did so strengthened to gale force. The rising wind and heavy seas soon had the effect they feared, for the tow-ropes parted once more. By now the *Fitzmaurice* was almost in sight of her goal, and having got the *Cleopatra* this far the crew were determined not to be beaten. Despite the heavy seas and the howling wind a boat was lowered, and after a long and difficult struggle they somehow managed to reconnect the hawsers. Just after 9 o'clock on that Wednesday evening, the *Fitzmaurice* proudly towed her prize into the safety of Ferrol harbour. For the *Cleopatra*, however, it was anything but a moment to be proud of for she was still lying on her beam ends, and thus was to suffer the indignity of having her bottom plates exposed to public view.

The following morning Captain Evans went ashore to see the British Vice-Consul resident in Ferrol and arranged to leave the *Cleopatra* in his custody. The Vice-Consul telegraphed the news to London where it arrived in time to save the Admiralty the trouble of deciding how to respond to Dixon's appeal. Interestingly, if the chain of communication had been quicker, Dixon might conceivably have heard of the *Cleopatra*'s rescue before he knew the full details of her abandonment, since the *Fitzmaurice* entered Ferrol harbour well over an hour before the *Olga* reached Falmouth. Her duty done, the *Fitzmaurice* then continued her voyage to Valencia. Here she unloaded the pig iron and picked up a cargo for Liverpool. On her arrival there in November the vessel was met by an anxious Captain Carter who went on board to see his opposite number. At Ferrol Evans had rather belatedly done his best to rescue the personal belongings of the *Cleopatra*'s crew, but he was too late as all their clothing and anything else of value had already been 'salvaged'. All that remained were the ship's log-book and some nautical instruments, including Carter's sextant. Of his luggage there was no trace. Gone was a collection of rare Greek and Roman coins, articles of sentimental value such as rings and lockets, and private papers. The only item which he was destined to see again was a pair of his cuff-links—and these were being worn by the hero of the salvage operation, the Chief Officer of the *Fitzmaurice*, who apparently had 'borrowed' them.

On receipt of the glad tidings of the *Cleopatra*'s safe arrival at Ferrol, John Dixon was naturally impatient to regain possession of her, but first he was going to have to settle the question of salvage with the owners of the *Fitzmaurice*—Messrs Burrell and Son of Glasgow. Accordingly, accompanied by Captain Carter, he caught a train for Scotland in the hope of settling the matter quickly. Unfortunately at their meeting Burrell insisted on a payment of £5,000 for services rendered, a sum far in excess of what Dixon considered reasonable. Patiently Dixon explained the unusual nature of his contract with Erasmus Wilson, and emphasised that the whole project had been undertaken in the national interest and was unlikely to lead to any profit. He then offered to write a cheque there and then for £600, but the shrewd Scotsman would not budge from the figure he had stated. General Alexander had been following events closely, and he wrote to his fellow Scot asking him to moderate his salvage claim since the *Fitzmaurice* had had the honour of saving the obelisk for the Nation. But despite this appeal to his patriotism and approaches made by other parties, Burrell would neither condescend to reduce his claim, nor to release the *Cleopatra*. The gulf between the two sides was so wide that it was obvious a court of law would need to settle the affair. So, pending the result of the litigation, Dixon put up bail in the Admiralty Court to the tune of £5,000 to enable the *Cleopatra* to continue her journey.

The salvage claim was heard in the Admiralty Division of the High Court in March and April 1878 by Sir R. J. Phillimore. Straight away Dixon admitted his liability to pay all salvage costs, and the reason for the court action was simply to decide on the amount he should pay. On the face of it the judge was confronted with a routine salvage case, since the fact that the *Cleopatra* had been purpose built to make this one specific voyage caused no complications. However, there was one serious stumbling block. The unique factor in this case was the cargo. How much was it worth? This thorny question needed to be settled, for the size of the salvage award depended on the values of both the vessel and its contents. In his affidavit Burrell contended that many European and American cities would be prepared to pay handsomely for the privilege of possessing a monument as rare and of such great antiquity as the obelisk, while on the other hand it appears to have been suggested by the other side, not too optimistically one feels, that it should be valued as a cargo of stone. Judge Phillimore had the unenviable job of deciding the exact value of the salvaged goods, as well as determining what proportion of this be awarded to the salvors.

When delivering his judgement Phillimore dwelt in detail on the bravery of the men from the *Fitzmaurice,* and on the antiquity of the obelisk. He also praised Dixon for his public spiritedness in undertaking the venture and regretted that this fact could in no way influence the decision of the court, for under the laws of salvage the crew of the *Fitzmaurice* had a right to be remunerated. The suggestion that the cargo should be considered merely as so many tons of granite was dismissed as being absurd, and Phillimore put it on a par with valuing a Michael Angelo sculpture in terms of the cost of the marble. In trying to assess the value of the cargo the only real precedent available was the £80,000 spent by the French nearly half a century earlier transporting the somewhat larger Luxor Obelisk to Paris, and after due deliberation Phillimore eventually settled on a figure of £25,000 for the total salvage value of the *Cleopatra* and her cargo. Obviously his valuation was really a shot in the dark, and *The Times* later criticised it as being far too high. The next thing was for him to assess the size of the salvage award, and here Phillimore had several factors to take into account. These were that the *Olga* had given up the search and completely abandoned the *Cleopatra* to the mercy of the elements, and the courage and skill repeatedly displayed by the crew of the *Fitzmaurice* in perilous circumstances. Bearing these points in mind, Phillimore had no hesitation in awarding the sum of £2,000 plus costs to the salvors. He also apportioned the award as follows: the owners — £1,200, Captain Evans — £250, and the remainder distributed amongst the crew according to their ratings, with a proviso that the volunteers who initially boarded the *Cleopatra* should receive double shares for rendering exceptional service.

At the beginning of December Captain Carter began making preparations to bring the *Cleopatra* over from Spain. First of all she would need refitting, so he bought several tons of material including rivets, nuts and bolts, lengths of chain etc, and then engaged a crew at Liverpool. The men were hand-picked with an eye to carrying out the necessary repairs as well as manning the *Cleopatra* during the seven hundred or so mile voyage from Ferrol to the Thames. His choice as mate was John Matthews, and the crew comprised John's brother Josiah, a riveter called Sam Nutland, two deckhands and a boy. The Matthews brothers were experienced seamen, and like Carter had spent years in the service of the P & O. Carter took passage at Liverpool aboard the *Nina*, a Spanish steamer, and arrived at

Ferrol with his crew and materials in time to take possession of the *Cleopatra* on 19 December, the date on which John Dixon secured her release by standing bail in the Admiralty Court. A thorough inspection of the vessel showed she was in remarkably good shape considering her experiences in the Bay of Biscay, for the hull had remained watertight. Above deck everything was in a shambles, thanks to the hurricane, but below deck all was in order, except of course for the iron rail ballast whose shifting had caused all the trouble. Three weeks later Carter and his men had repaired the rudder, fitted a new tiller, stepped a new mast, fitted new sails and rigging, and, most important of all, had this time made absolutely sure that the ballast could not break free.

Before sailing for Ferrol Captain Carter had assisted John Dixon to make arrangements for towing the *Cleopatra* on the last leg of her voyage to the Thames. The owners of the *Olga* were prepared to complete the tow, but as this would have meant waiting to suit their convenience, Dixon felt obliged to make other arrangements. A member of Parliament, James Lloyd Ashley, generously offered the services of his 360 ton private steam yacht, *Eothen*, but Dixon politely declined. Apparently he had decided it would be more prudent to let experts handle the job rather than leave it to amateurs. No doubt he was helped in this decision by adverse comment in some sections of the press which blamed him for the tragedy in the Bay of Biscay. It had been alleged that he should shoulder some of the blame because he had tried to save money by hiring a cargo ship to tow the *Cleopatra* from Alexandria. Obviously any businessman worth his salt rates cost as an important consideration, but Dixon and Carter had also satisfied themselves that the *Olga* was capable of towing the *Cleopatra* at her design speed of six knots. Perhaps a deep-sea tug would have been more suitable, but even she would have been compelled to slip her tow in the fierce gale which struck the *Olga*. The unanswerable question is whether lives would have still been lost. At any rate Dixon decided to play safe, and he contacted William Watkins who owned some of the largest and most powerful tugs in the Port of London. The pride of the fleet was the *Anglia*, a three funnelled paddle tug with a crew of seventeen hands plus two captains. Captain John Tracy looked after the normal navigation while Captain David Glue was responsible for towing operations. The *Anglia* had earned a good reputation for ocean towing since her launching in 1866, having brought many crippled vessels back home from places as far away as Port Said and St Helena. Dixon engaged the *Anglia* for the job and signed a contract with Watkins under which £500 would be paid, if, and when, the *Cleopatra* reached her destination.

This time no chances were to be taken with the weather. Dixon had decided that towing should not be resumed until conditions looked favourable, and he arranged for the Meteorological Department in Britain to supply daily forecasts. These were supplemented by American weather details generously telegraphed across the Atlantic by the *New York Herald*. The full moon was due on 19 January, and as this was usually reckoned to be a favourable time for a voyage up the English Channel the departure was provisionally fixed for the 16th. Accordingly the *Anglia* sailed from the Thames on the morning of 8 January carrying several young passengers who were eagerly looking forward to the excitement of the round trip. These were Watkins's two sons John and Philip, who were accompanied by their cousin Alfred. Also on board, but for business not pleasure, was a journalist. After an uneventful voyage the *Anglia* reached Ferrol four days later where Captain Carter and the refitted *Cleopatra* eagerly awaited her arrival. Within two days all the preparations for the voyage home had been completed, and when the three captains met on board the *Anglia* on

36 Leaving Ferrol. The paddle tug *Anglia* towing the *Cleopatra* out of the Spanish port of Ferrol just after dawn on Tuesday 15 January 1878.(*The Illustrated London News*, 1878).

14 January to examine the latest weather forecasts they were delighted to find that the outlook was unusually promising. The prospect of a period of settled weather was too good to miss, so they decided to leave early next day on the morning tide, twenty-four hours ahead of schedule.

At 7.00am on Tuesday 15 January Captain Carter signalled to the *Anglia* that he was ready for departure. The two vessels lay expectantly at anchor in the middle of the harbour connected together by a short length of fifteen inch hawser, but hidden from each other by the darkness which precedes the dawn. Just after 7.30am both vessels weighed their anchors, and although the sun had not yet risen there were a few streaks of light showing over the hills to the east, and everyone was predicting a calm cloudless morning. Ten minutes later the *Anglia* slowly moved ahead taking up the small amount of slack in the tow-rope, and immediately great difficulty was experienced in towing the *Cleopatra* since she insisted on sheering to port. Under the control of a Spanish pilot the *Anglia* slowly felt her way through the harbour in the half light of dawn towards the entrance and its protecting fortresses. Before she got there the *Cleopatra* yawed so violently that her bow came level with the stern of the *Anglia*, but there was no immediate danger as the *Cleopatra* was well clear on the port quarter with the short hawser at full stretch. Luckily there were few vessels about and there was plenty of room for manoeuvring in the outer harbour; even so there were no doubt a few eye-brows raised at the antics of the *Cleopatra* as she cavorted first to port, then to starboard, like an over-excited dog straining at the leash. Soon, by judicious use of her powerful engines and alterations in course, the *Anglia* managed to get the *Cleopatra* under control.

By 9am the pilot had been dropped and they were rounding Cape Priano where the ocean swell began to make itself felt. The *Cleopatra* responded by again sheering wildly to port, and then, when checked by the hawser, across to starboard, as though objecting to the short leash on which she was still held. Gradually the crew of the *Anglia* paid out more of the hawser over the tow-rail at the stern of their ship, and when the full one hundred fathoms stretched between the two vessels the *Cleopatra* began to settle down and steer better. Soon they were out in the open sea making a steady five knots. The yawing motion had now disappeared and instead the *Cleopatra* was observing her usual routine of pitching heavily, and even though the swell was not excessive she occasionally dipped her bows right under. As Carter later told a reporter from *The Times*, 'she pitches a good deal, plunging sometimes like a porpoise, with all but her cabin under water, then she jumps up again from her dip like a diving duck.'[3]

At noon the light north-east wind was beginning to freshen and there were heavy clouds building up on the horizon. Before long the sea was rising and the *Anglia* signalled on her blackboard to see if Carter wished to turn back. He preferred to go on, and although for several hours they were down to half speed coping with a strong east wind on the starboard quarter, by dusk the wind had moderated and the swell had subsided. That night as the moon occasionally broke through the cloud cover to check on their progress, the *Anglia* steamed steadily on northwards towards Ushant and the English Channel.

When Wednesday dawned the weather was unaltered and soon Captain Carter was chalking on his blackboard 'Faster if like' and aboard the *Anglia* Captain Glue obliged. They plodded on—their track lay rather to the east of the main sailing routes—and they hardly sighted a sail all day. At sunset although the broken cloud persisted there was virtually no wind and almost a flat calm. Shortly after midnight the *Cleopatra* had a spell of steering badly and Carter burnt a white light to request the *Anglia* to go slower, but just after dawn speed was increased again to six knots. Incredibly, for the Bay of Biscay in January, the fine weather still held and showed no signs of breaking. As was her habit the *Cleopatra* insisted on pitching somewhat even though the water was as flat as a mill-pond, but despite this Carter was naturally delighted with their good fortune. The voyage in fact was beginning to become monotonous, and good humoured messages were passed back and forth between the two ships on their blackboards as they tried to pass the long hours of idleness. Alfred Watkins recorded one such conversation:

Cleopatra signals "Will you dine with me?"
Anglia, "Excuse me."
Cleopatra, "Roast beef, hare, jelly, plum-pudding, and mince-pies."
Anglia, "Will dine off your fowls." [Some live fowls belonging to Captain Carter were on board the *Anglia.*]
Cleopatra, "I shall want my fowls."[4]

Shortly after dusk on the Thursday the *Cleopatra* lit blue and red lights to warn the

37 Stopping for repairs. The two vessels hove-to in the English Channel while repairs to the *Cleopatra's* rudder were carried out.(*The Illustrated London News*, 1878).

Anglia that she was running in towards the shore, but Carter need not have worried for an immediate reply on her steam whistle and the fact that the *Anglia* was already turning to port showed all was well. Just before midnight they sighted the Ushant Light and then in the early hours of Friday morning rounded the north-west tip of France and entered the English Channel. Half of the 700 mile voyage from Ferrol was now behind them, and they were all more than pleased to have had such an easy passage across the Bay of Biscay.

Around midday they hove to for half an hour while repairs were carried out on the *Cleopatra's* steering. Two hours later it was out of action again and thereafter the *Cleopatra* was hauled along with a permanent yaw to port. Luckily the fine weather persisted and did not break until they had nearly reached the safety of the Thames, and so long as the sea remained as smooth as glass the lack of steering did not really matter since the fifteen inch tow-line could cope quite happily with the extra strain. At 8.30pm they passed Start Point in Devon, and twelve hours later off Portland Bill made their first direct contact with another vessel, a pilot cutter. The pilot was given a sovereign to pay for a telegram informing John Dixon of their progress. He was also given a bottle of whisky for his trouble, and perhaps he sampled his present too liberally for the telegram never arrived. However, as the *Anglia* steamed on her way up channel an observant coastguard reported their presence.

During the Saturday night the wind began to freshen and it gradually increased in strength all Sunday morning. By noon as the two vessels came abreast of Dover the wind was veering from the west round to the south as though intent on following them around the south-eastern corner of England. Soon half a gale was blowing and heavy rain clouds threatened. By dusk they had rounded the North Foreland and leaving Margate astern headed east up into the relative shelter of the Thames Estuary. Well before midnight the *Anglia* and *Cleopatra* lay safely at anchor off the Chapman Light near Southend.

Early the next morning, Monday 21 January, the *Anglia* was on her way again with the *Cleopatra* obediently keeping station astern. Just after 10.00am they moored at a buoy off

Gravesend. Ashore Mr and Mrs John Dixon were impatiently waiting to come aboard the *Anglia* in order to congratulate the captains and crews of the two vessels. While the happy reunion was taking place the Dixon's pleasure was enhanced by a telegram which arrived from Osborne on the Isle of Wight. It was addressed personally to John Dixon, and in it Queen Victoria expressed her pleasure at the safe arrival of the Cleopatra's Needle.

After receiving customs clearance the two vessels left Gravesend at around 1pm and continued on their way up river. This time the *Cleopatra* followed hard on the heels of the *Anglia* as the tow-rope had been shortened to fifteen fathoms (about the same length as the *Cleopatra* herself) in order to try and keep her under control in the narrowing waterway. The pilot seems to have had a more sensitive touch than his Spanish counterpart, for little trouble was experienced due to the *Cleopatra* sheering. An hour or so after leaving Gravesend they had ascended as far as Woolwich on the flood tide. As they passed the training ships *Cornwall* and *Chichester* the boys manned the yards and cheering lustily waved their caps in salute—a greeting appreciated by the *Anglia* and *Cleopatra* who both dipped their ensigns in acknowledgement. On both banks the wharves and piers were thronged with groups of spectators who cheered their progress. Approaching Blackwall the crowds increased, and so did the traffic on the river. By now the pilot and the captains of the two vessels were having to call upon all their experience and skill. Not only was the *Cleopatra* potentially a hazard to other ships using the busy waterway, but inevitably many

38 Arrival at Gravesend. The *Cleopatra* moored at Gravesend on the morning of Monday 21 January 1878 waiting for a jubilant John Dixon to come aboard.(*The Illustrated London News*, 1878).

small craft seemed oblivious of the risks they were taking when they made a close inspection of this unusual vessel. In mid-afternoon the *Anglia* gladly handed over her charge to a smaller tug, the *Mosquito,* at the narrow entrance to the East India Docks. By 5pm the *Cleopatra* had been safely manoeuvred inside and was snugly moored in one of the best berths in the East India Export Dock, which had been liberally provided free of charge by the dock owners.

6

Adelphi Steps

When the *Cleopatra* arrived on the Thames in January 1878 a firm decision had still not been taken as to where the obelisk should be erected. Over fifty years had now passed since it was originally presented to Britain by Mehemet Ali in 1820, and during that time various places had been proposed as its new home including Trafalgar Square and Hyde Park. Then, General Alexander had entered the arena to champion the cause of the Cleopatra's Needle, and in 1872 he persuaded the Metropolitan Board of Works to grant him a site— the centre of a two acre ornamental garden on the Thames Embankment at the bottom of Northumberland Avenue. Four years later John Dixon and Erasmus Wilson joined forces to bring the Cleopatra's Needle to Britain, and with happy prospect of the impending arrival of the obelisk there had begun what *The Times* later aptly referred to as the 'Battle of the Sites.'

The battle was still being fought when the obelisk reached London, and for over nine months the press had been full of letters, articles, and even editorials on the subject; literally dozens of different sites having been put forward for consideration. Every armchair pundit seemed to have his own idea, and even the experts couldn't agree. Most of the opposing forces were split into various camps depending on what they believed to be the correct siting of an obelisk. Some people favoured an open site where it could stand in isolation well away from buildings and be seen from a distance silhouetted against the skyline, such as somewhere in St James's Park, or Green Park, or Hyde Park, or even on a purpose built artificial island in the middle of the Round Pond in Kensington Gardens. Another faction took the opposite viewpoint and stated categorically that the obelisk must be placed in close proximity to buildings, for after all the Egyptians had always erected them at the entrances of temples. In any case, they argued, in the open when viewed from a distance it would be indistinguishable from the many church spires and chimneys of breweries etc, which dotted the capital. The most popular of these sites was the forecourt of the British Museum, although the top of Ludgate Hill by the entrance to St Paul's Cathedral had its supporters, as did Greenwich Hospital. A third group adopted a more balanced viewpoint. Its members believed that the obelisk should have room to breathe and yet should be visible from a distance against a background which included buildings tall enough to give it scale, but not so large as to dwarf it. They tended to favour the open spaces formed at the junctions of London's major streets, down which the needle would be seen from afar. One proposal was Regent's Circus (ie Piccadilly Circus), but for many the ideal position was Parliament Square.

However, many military men looked upon the obelisk as being a truly fitting memorial to the glorious victories won by the British Navy and Army against the French at

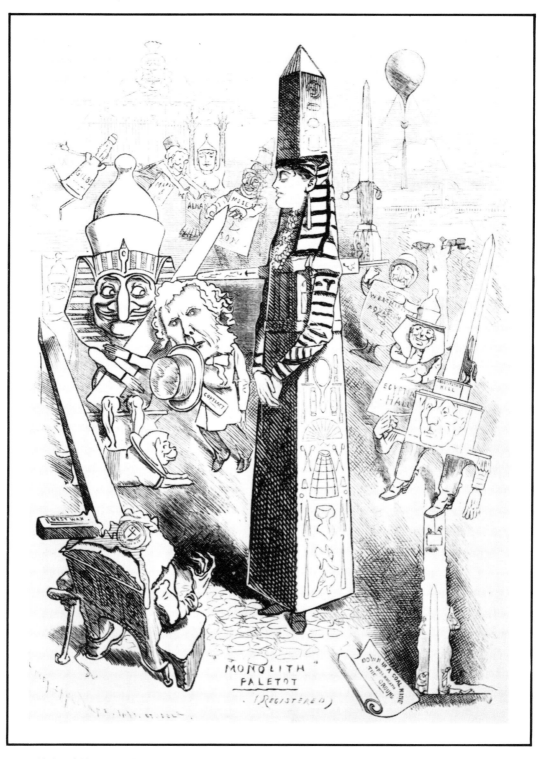

MONOLITH
PALETOT
(REGISTERED)

39 A Sight of Sites. *Punch*'s suggestions as to where the perplexed Wilson should site the Cleopatra's Needle ranged from the absurd to the ridiculous. Why not put it down a coal-mine or raise it aloft with a balloon?*(Punch, 1877).*

40 The proposed site in St James's Park. General Alexander's choice of home for the Cleopatra's Needle lay just inside the railing of St James's Park. He visualised it forming a fitting memorial to the British victories over the French at Alexandria, and appropriately the spot he preferred was within sight of the Admiralty and Horse Guards.(*The Engineer*, 1878).

Alexandria nearly eighty years before. They visualised it being mounted on a suitably inscribed base, and indeed detailed plans for the undertaking were drawn up by a London architect. Not surprisingly General Alexander was one of the leading promoters of the scheme. The spot he preferred lay just inside St James's Park, appropriately in full view of both the Admiralty and the Horse Guards. Backers of this scheme were not exclusively military men, and they included Alderman Cotton and Charles Barry, the President of the Royal Institute of British Architects.

The final choice of site, subject of course to the approval of the Metropolitan Board of Works, lay in the hands of the two men who were primarily responsible for the venture, and fortunately John Dixon and Erasmus Wilson were in agreement. They both preferred Parliament Square, and so did Waynman Dixon. Originally when the contract was signed in January 1877 it was their intention to erect the obelisk on the Thames Embankment,

41 The proposed site in Parliament Square. The site favoured by John Dixon and Erasmus Wilson was in front of the Houses of Parliament. Their plans to erect the needle there were foiled by the obstructiveness of the directors of the Metropolitan District Railway whose underground line passed directly beneath the chosen position.(*The Illustrated London News*, 1877).

and the specific site they had in mind was the one at the end of Northumberland Avenue granted for the purpose to General Alexander some years earlier. However, on a closer examination Dixon was less enthusiastic, since Hungerford Railway Bridge lay within fifty feet. Then when he discovered future building plans for the area included an adjacent ten storey hotel he concluded that unless a better site was available 'I should feel sorry I had ever unearthed the obelisk from the sands of Egypt.'[1] So much for the official site. On examining other riverside locations Dixon found to his dismay that at most of them extensive foundation work would be required to support the needle, and that even then the sites were far from ideal due to neighbouring buildings or bridges spoiling the prospect. He therefore looked further afield and soon decided in favour of Parliament Square.

As the summer of 1877 progressed, so did opposition to the Parliament Square site, and Dixon decided to try and convince the sceptics. At his own expense a full-sized painted wooden replica of the Cleopatra's Needle was erected at the chosen spot near to the statues of politicians Lord Palmerston and the Earl of Derby. This quickly evoked comment in Parliament, where as usual opinion was fairly evenly divided. Elsewhere the reactions were also mixed. For instance architect Charles Barry, whose father had designed the new Houses of Parliament, thought siting the obelisk in such a setting would be an artistic blunder, yet his fellow architects Sir Gilbert Scott and Edmund Street were but two of the many influential men who disagreed with this point of view. More crucial was the opinion of the Directors of the Metropolitan District Railway whose underground line passed directly beneath the site. Apparently they feared the vibrations set up by their trains would one day encourage the needle to drop into the tunnel. The engineer responsible for constructing the railway was John Fowler, and he tried to allay their fears by assuring them there would be no danger if iron beams were used to stiffen the tunnel roof when constructing the foundations for the obelisk. Despite this the Directors were far from happy, and they demanded a perpetual indemnity against the needle causing a railway accident. This was something that neither John Dixon nor any insurance company could possibly provide. At the end of January 1878 with the Cleopatra's Needle patiently waiting to take up residence Dixon was forced to admit defeat and the plans for Parliament Square were abandoned.

It quickly transpired that the St James's Park site favoured by General Alexander was also unavailable. Since John Dixon was personally liable for any additional expenses involved he was naturally unwilling to move the obelisk very far from the river. Although he desired to see this 'noble relic of ancient engineering skill' placed in a worthy site, he publicly announced that he was 'not disposed to incur the odium of annoying the public by interrupting the traffic of leading London thoroughfares and expending a further £10,000

42 A peep into the interior. Some intrepid explorers intent on examining the needle's hieroglyphics crawling inside the *Cleopatra* as she lay in the East India Docks. *(The Graphic,* 1878).

for the sake of depositing it at the British Museum.'[2] Virtually all the other possible locations were also ruled out for various reasons, and Dixon once more turned to the Thames Embankment for an answer to his problem. A closer inspection revealed that one position was superior to all others, namely the Adelphi Steps, midway between Hungerford and Waterloo Bridges, and directly across the river from the site now occupied by the Royal Festival Hall. After obtaining Wilson's approval Dixon announced his decision in a letter to *The Times* and extolled the virtues of Adelphi Steps as follows:

This is a fine site. The foundations are good, the splendid grey granite mass of the Embankment, the solid grandeur of Waterloo Bridge, the distant background of Somerset-house, the river, and the Adelphi-gardens form appropriate surroundings that will, I trust, commend the selection to the approbation of the public. The obelisk there will be visible along the whole line of the Embankment, but will be seen to greatest advantage on approaching from Westminster.[3]

Within ten days of the announcement the wooden model of the obelisk had been dismantled and re-erected at Adelphi Steps, to enable the members of the Metropolitan Board of Works to assess for themselves the suitability of the site. At a meeting held on 15 February they unanimously endorsed John Dixon's choice. So ended the Battle of the Sites.

After her arrival on the Thames the *Cleopatra* remained in the East India Docks for two weeks. The vessel was thrown open to the public and hundreds came to see this strange little craft. Some venturesome souls even begged permission to be allowed to crawl around in the interior to examine her precious cargo. Despite it being only a few minutes walk from Poplar Station on the Blackwell Railway, the docks were not the most convenient of places to put the *Cleopatra* on show, so Dixon made arrangements with the Thames Conservancy Board for her to be towed up river and moored off St Thomas's Hospital, just across the river from the Houses of Parliament.

On the morning of Saturday 2 February the *Cleopatra*, with Captain Carter aboard, was hauled back out into the Thames by Watkins's diminutive tug *Era*. As the *Cleopatra* passed through the massive dock gates she was greeted by her escort, *Ajax* and *Trojan*, two larger tugs owned by Messrs Page and East. Due to the *Cleopatra*'s propensity for yawing wildly and unexpectedly, John Dixon was taking no chances on the short trip up the narrowing and crowded waterway to Westminster, so instead of being treated like an honoured guest, the *Cleopatra* was to make the journey like a dangerous prisoner under guard, with the tugs closely shackled one on each side of her. Because of the bridges the *Cleopatra* was minus her mast, but she still managed to proudly display the Union Jack, the Red Ensign, and the burgee with her name on it, as well as sporting a mass of bunting. The tugs were also gaily dressed for the occasion, flying their house flags, the Royal Standard, and the flag of the Shipwright's Company. Alexander and John Dixon were aboard one of the tugs in the company of many guests. The Lord Mayor had sent his apologies and a representative, who together with the President of the Board of Trade, headed the cast. Other vessels also joined in to form a procession which was led by a steamer belonging to the Thames Conservancy Board. The flotilla slowly came up river on the flood tide, and the passage of only four miles was by no means plain sailing, especially in the Pool of London around Wapping, due to the busy state of the Thames. All told this short trip took over two hours, and was made to the cheers of crowds of spectators who lined the bridges and banks. The atmosphere was enhanced by the salutes fired from some of the wharves. Just before 2pm the *Cleopatra* was safely moored off St Thomas's Hospital about one hundred yards above Westminster Bridge.

On the Sunday the Embankment and Westminster Bridge were thronged with Londoners who from dawn till dusk flocked to see the capital's latest novelty. Local watermen were kept busy charging threepence a head to row people around the *Cleopatra*. Strange stories circulated amongst the crowd. It was rumoured that the needle had broken during the voyage. Some believed it was made of rock crystal, others of marble. Some obviously only had a vague idea of what was hidden from view in the cylindrical hull of the *Cleopatra*, and others had strange notions of where it had come from. The weather was cold, but there was a holiday atmosphere. Pedlars were there by the dozen with merchandise to meet every need, and some were busy hawking instant penny pamphlets on the needle and threepenny booklets (including one by Erasmus Wilson) to the eager public.

From Monday morning a steady stream of visitors was allowed on board where several plates had been removed from the deck to enable them to gaze upon the needle lying snugly in its case. Admission was free—the general public being allowed on board daily up to 2pm, after which access was by invitation only. Ideally a berth where they could have boarded her by a gangway would have been best, but there was a shortage of such places

43 Westminster. The *Cleopatra* moored off St Thomas's Hospital in February 1878 where she quickly became a popular tourist attraction. In the background are the Houses of Parliament and Westminster Bridge.(*The Illustrated London News*, 1878).

in central London, visitors had to be content with paying a boatman for the pleasure of being rowed out to the *Cleopatra*. Visiting her quickly became the fashionable thing to do, and during the three months she remained at her moorings waiting for the site at Adelphi Steps to be prepared, many of the local watermen were kept lucratively employed.

Adelphi Steps had formerly been a popular point of disembarkation from the multitude of river steamers which at one time plied the Thames providing a convenient form of transport, but latterly this role had been usurped by the railways. Two separate flights of steps led up from the river, and just below road level they met a platform which jutted out from the Victoria Embankment. It was in the centre of this platform that the Cleopatra's Needle was to be erected. The Metropolitan Board of Works had discovered that they would need further powers to permit them to accept the needle, so a bill was presented to Parliament and quickly passed through. Under *The Monuments(Metropolis) Act, 1878* these powers were granted. The Act specifically vested control of the obelisk in the hands of the Board, and amongst other provisions was one for a fine, not exceeding £5, for the offences of posting bills upon the needle or defacing it.

Beneath the chosen position were four large arches, so the site was obviously going to need strengthening to enable it to take the weight of the needle and its pedestal. Work began in the middle of March. First of all concrete was poured in to form a strong raft underneath the arches resting securely on the tenacious London clay, and then the arches themselves were completely filled with concrete, providing a huge solid base for the needle. The two flights of steps were retained as they conveniently formed supporting buttresses. All told some 6,000 cubic yards of concrete are reported to have been used, weighing many thousands of tons. This part of the operation took two months, and it appears that true to their word, the Metropolitan Board of Works ungraciously allowed John Dixon the privilege of paying for these alterations to the Embankment, for their willingness to accept the obelisk was it seems not matched by their generosity.

The *Cleopatra* remained at her moorings off St Thomas's Hospital for the best part of four months. Early on the morning of Thursday 30 May Captain Carter, faithful to the end, was preparing his strange craft for her final cruise, the half mile back down river to Adelphi Steps. Also aboard were the Matthews brothers. After two tugs had been closely shackled alongside, the *Cleopatra* was turned around to face downriver. By 10.30am all was ready. As is usual on such occasions *The Times* had a man on the spot to report how

. . . the beautiful Egyptian Queen's uncomely namesake was gallantly escorted down the Thames by the *Era* and *Trojan* under their respective Captains, Palmer and Smith. The waterway was kept clear by an officer of the Thames Conservancy. Meanwhile crowds clustered on the Albert Embankment, and still more thickly on Westminster Bridge, through the third arch of which from the north bank the flotilla steamed at 10.42, Mr. J. Dixon, having already hailed Captain Carter from the west parapet, urging him to keep the *Cleopatra*'s deck as clear as possible. On reaching Whitehall gardens, about 10.45, a chain of coal-barges came across her path, but with a little devious steering the obstruction was cleared, and by 11 the Adelphi-steps were reached.[4]

At the foot of the western flight of steps a timber cradle had been securely fixed to the river bed with the intention of floating the *Cleopatra* onto it at high tide. She had arrived with two hours to spare, and as they waited a little offshore Carter could see the water level slowly creeping its way up the marker post. By high tide it had settled just above the desired level, but the margin of reserve was small, so John Dixon cautiously decided to wait twenty-four hours until a higher tide was due. Overnight the vessel was lightened as much as was humanly possible, reducing her draught a few more inches, and early on the following afternoon she glided into the cradle to be left high and dry seven feet above the river bed when the tide ebbed. The time had now come for Captain Carter to bid farewell to his ungainly and unruly craft, and to hand her over to the site manager, George Double.

The wooden replica of the obelisk had long since been removed from the top of Adelphi Steps. It had only stood there for a couple of weeks, for once it had served its purpose the wooden needle had been dismantled during the last week of February. Now that the *Cleopatra* was resting firmly on her cradle, the preparations for removing the needle from its case could begin. First the cabin and the rest of the superstructure were removed, then the cylindrical shell was rotated through a quarter of a turn so as to bring the best preserved face of the obelisk around to face the roadway. The next job was to strip off the top half of the iron plating and cut away the upper portions of all the frames and bulkheads. By 12 June this phase of the work had been completed and once more Cleopatra's Needle lay exposed to public view. Throughout the summer crowds flocked to the scene:

The pavement of the Victoria Embankment on both sides of the Adelphi-steps is daily lined with a considerable crowd, watching with keen interest the gradual disintegration of the monolith-ship *Cleopatra*, and the simultaneous rising of the solid structure of Penrhyn granite which will before long relieve it of its grandly historical freight, and be the permanent resting-place of the obelisk. Very few visitors were admitted, and these by card only within the hoarding. . . . With such rare exceptions the area within the enclosure is jealously guarded by policemen as the peculiar domain of Mr. Double, who is superintending the work on Mr. Dixon's behalf, while Mr. Broom represents the Metropolitan Board of Works. On Whit Tuesday a visitors' book was opened, and among the first entries were names from Toronto and Melbourne, as well as that of Professor Erasmus Wilson.[5]

Among the many distinguished visitors were the Prince and Princess of Wales, and the Prime Minister, Lord Beaconsfield. The Prime Minister came straight from his office just after 7pm one evening in August and spent some considerable time discussing with John Dixon the intricacies of erecting the obelisk.

On 13 June a pair of Tangye's hydraulic jacks were placed under the butt of the needle, and early the following morning a trial lift was carried out raising the end a couple of inches. Satisfied with the result George Double then proceeded to position three more pairs of jacks, one near the other end of the needle, and two beneath its centre. All was now ready to extract the obelisk from the shattered remnants of its casing. As the huge monolith was slowly inched up by the jacks successive layers of timber packing were placed beneath it. When the needle had been lifted clear of the ironwork, four screw traversers were brought into action with the object of dragging it up the steps. The faces of the obelisk had been protected by a wooden coating and it was to make the ascent pointed end first. Each traverser consisted of a four inch diameter steel screw which was wound in by four men straining on levers. By a combination of the vertical lift provided by the hydraulic jacks, and the horizontal pull of the traversers, the needle gradually climbed the stairs. Frequently it was gently lowered back onto an extra layer of wooden packing, and after the jacks and traversers had been repositioned, the needle would resume its slow ascent. By 22 June the obelisk had been lifted several feet vertically and seven feet eastwards. A week later the corresponding distances were six feet and twenty-five feet respectively. At first

44 The end of the *Cleopatra*. Workmen breaking the *Cleopatra* up on 6 July as she rests on her cradle at the foot of Adelphi Steps. This water-colour by John Dixon captures the tragic scene, for sadly once she had completed her mission the *Cleopatra*'s only value was as scrap iron.

progress was slow as work could only be carried out at low tide, but once the needle had climbed out of reach of the water it was able to ascend at a much faster rate. Eventually after being traversed over one hundred feet and raised nearly thirty feet the Cleopatra's Needle had mounted the flight of steps and was resting on the platform.

Once the needle was well clear, a gang of men descended upon what was left of the *Cleopatra* to break her up. She lay helpless on the cradle with the broken ends of her frames pointing forlornly skywards like the bones of a gutted fish, and sadly, now that her mission was accomplished, her only value was as scrap iron. Throughout June stonemasons had been busily laying four courses of granite blocks to form a base upon which the obelisk's pedestal was ultimately to be built, and by mid-July the needle was suspended horizontally on timber baulks with its centre of gravity directly over the middle of the granite base. The masons had also partially dressed square the butt of the obelisk, for the Romans had cut into it to accommodate their bronze crabs. John Dixon intended mounting the Cleopatra's Needle directly on its pedestal, since calculations had shown that there was no danger of a gale toppling it, even if the wind force exceeded that of a hurricane.

45 Lifting the horizontal needle. The massive timber framework nears completion in late July 1878.

46 Lifting the horizontal needle in early August 1878. Spectators pausing in their stroll to watch the final preparations for the lifting operation. In the foreground a disappointed barrow-boy receives his marching orders.

A wrought iron jacket designed by Benjamin Baker had been forged in four separate pieces by the Thames Iron Works, Blackwall, and this was now assembled around the middle of the needle. The jacket was twenty feet long and was fitted with knife-edge trunnions carefully positioned so that the obelisk would freely pivot about them like the beam of a gigantic pair of scales. During the second half of July and early August a massive timber framework, well over fifty feet high, and securely braced on all sides by inclined struts, was erected such that half of it stood on each side of the horizontal needle. The intention was to raise it aloft between the two halves of the framework using hydraulic jacks. Two iron box beams lay alongside the obelisk, one on each side, and the jacket trunnions rested upon them. In a four week period beginning on 7 August the iron beams were ponderously hoisted up in the air by the hydraulic jacks, and thus the horizontal monolith was gradually lifted high enough for swinging into the vertical position. Each four inch lift of the jacks took a mere ten minutes, and after timber packing had been inserted the needle was carefully lowered a fraction of an inch to rest upon it. The jacks themselves were then packed up four inches higher ready to commence the next lift. All told the daily average was five or six lifting operations and apart from brief delays caused by storms the lifting continued steadily, day in day out, except of course for the Sabbath, until on Saturday 7 September the needle had been raised the required 48 feet. The stone

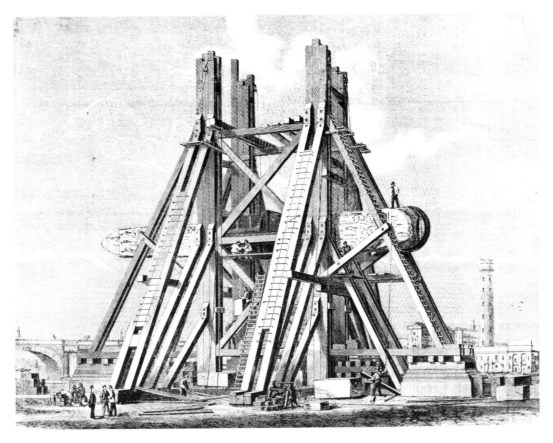

47 By late August 1878 the huge monolith had been lifted to the half-way mark.(*Engineering*, 1878).

pedestal had been finished several days earlier by masons bravely working directly beneath the obelisk during the lifting operation.

At last it was possible for John Dixon to fix a date for the final acts of swinging the obelisk into the vertical position and lowering it onto its pedestal, and he announced to the press that the ceremony would begin at 3pm on Thursday 12 September. The days leading up to this fateful hour, when his reputation as an engineer would be on public trial, were no doubt tinged with anxiety for John Dixon, since the operation was, to say the least, a novel one. The time passed making final preparations, checking everything was in order, and generally tidying up the site. To control the needle while swinging it, steel restraining cables were fastened to each end, and the free ends of the cables led to winches. On 11 September the latches which securely held the pivoted monolith in the horizontal position were released so that the operation could be rehearsed. So finely balanced was the needle about its centre of gravity that John Dixon found he could easily swing the massive beam by his own exertions. Satisfied that this augured well for the morrow he ordered George Double to relock the obelisk in the horizontal position.

Large crowds were expected to attend, so arrangements had been made for the Metropolitan Police to regulate traffic and preserve law and order. On Thursday, well before the ceremony was due to begin, the Superintendent of E Division had arrived with three inspectors, fifteen sergeants, and 150 constables. The inevitable reporter from *The*

48 Lifting the horizontal needle. Workmen posing for a photographer in September 1878 as he records for posterity the arrival of the Cleopatra's Needle at the top of the timber framework.

Times was also present to capture the scene for the readers of his newspaper.

Between 1 and 2 o'clock a heavy downpour of rain proved more effectual in scattering the gathering crowd than any fear of the police. But after an hour or so of decidedly bad weather there was a gradual return of sunshine, and behind the line of constables barricading the Embankment some few thousands of people clustered and watched what was going on with the keenest interest. The pavement of Adelphi terrace was densely thronged, and there were many eager spectators on Waterloo-bridge. For long distances on both sides the river pavement of the Embankment was crowded. From an early hour the *Duke of Connaught* steamer was on its station off the Adelphi-steps, the guests of Mr. Dixon and Professor Erasmus Wilson, reinforced by members of the Metropolitan Board of Works, being conveyed on board its tender the *Prince of Wales* from Westminster Pier at short intervals until the large vessel became almost overloaded. Several small steamers were also in waiting, freighted with full cargoes of earnest sightseers. Four Thames Police boats and a Thames Conservancy boat kept the water way, and the flag of the Port Medical Officer floated from his steam launch.[6]

Within the hoarding surrounding the site were John Dixon, Benjamin Baker, and George Double, plus of course the workmen who had been detailed for the various duties involved. A few privileged guests had also been admitted, notably Erasmus Wilson, Henry Carter, Henry Palfrey Stephenson, and Sir Joseph Bazalgette who was the Chief Engineer of the Metropolitan Board of Works. General Alexander was aboard the *Duke of Connaught,* from where he was to get a grandstand view of the whole operation. While waiting he looked up at the Cleopatra's Needle towering above him, 'and viewed it from the deck, with considerable emotion, suspended in mid-air, whilst reflecting on all the anxiety and trouble, and expenditure of time and means it had occasioned, but extremely thankful withal to see at length the accomplishment of the dream of ten years.'[7] Of those mainly instrumental in making the occasion possible, the only absentee was Waynman Dixon, who unfortunately was out of the country on business.

Of the ceremony which accompanied the installation of the stone there is little to say, because practically there was none. The Prince of Wales, who had signified his willingness to attend, was unable to do so until a much later period, and the responsibility of leaving the massive stone supported high above the ground for an indefinite time was too great to justify Mr. Dixon in delay.[8]

The undertaking was no every-day task, such as any civil engineer could manage offhand but, as an adept in the profession, who was watching it with the liveliest interest, observed, the first time in engineering experience that anything approaching 200 tons had been carried on iron knife-edges. The tackle was worked by a pair of winches at each end, which five minutes before 3 were manned by three men each, making a dozen in all. A minute or two before the hour, the Needle having been unlocked, as in the previous day's rehearsal, the winches began to turn, and the huge monolith's motion was almost instantaneously perceptible, as the thin end left behind it a chock of timber on which it had rested. At 3.10pm the obelisk was already at an angle of about 45 degrees, considered a most critical juncture, and at the end of five minutes more, 60 degrees was reached. By the time the half-hour had chimed from the Clock Tower [of Big Ben] the rose granite single-stone spire of the grand old Pharaoh Thothmes III, had, to any save a mathematical eye, taken an upright position.[9]

The needle was now suspended vertically above its pedestal with a gap of about four inches between them. Doubts were raised as to whether or not the obelisk was truly perpendicular, so after some discussion with the other engineers, Dixon decided to postpone lowering the needle onto its support until the following morning. Wooden

49 Erection of the obelisk. Four views depicting the operations. *Bottom*—the horizontal needle ready and waiting on Wednesday 11 September 1878. *Top-left*—workmen manning one of the winches just before 3pm on the Thursday. *Top-right*—by 3.10pm the obelisk had been swung through 45⁰. *Centre*—on the morning of Friday 13 September the huge stone was carefully lowered onto its pedestal.*(The Illustrated London News, 1878).*

wedges were therefore inserted between the obelisk and pedestal, and the cables were examined to ensure their tightness. Meanwhile the crowd, which had watched the swinging operation in respectful silence, had been good naturedly waiting for the final act to be performed. As the news of the postponement spread, just before four o'clock they

burst forth in ringing cheers, which were renewed from river, road, terrace, and bridge as the Union Jack was run up on the flagstaff which overtopped the pyramidion on the north side, and again when the Egyptian (Turkish) flag followed on the south. These cheers for the colours were in honour of the Queen and Khedive; but the first burst was for Mr. Dixon and his coadjutors, and in recognition of a great triumph already won.[10]

After making absolutely certain that the obelisk was secure John Dixon went aboard the *Duke of Connaught* to join his guests, who heartily congratulated him on his achievement. Speeches were made and healths were drunk and eventually after a long festive evening the party broke up. No doubt it was a happy John Dixon who retired for the night, and his pleasure at having succeeded in his ambition to bring the Cleopatra's Needle to Britain was crowned during the next few days by the many telegrams of congratulations he received. These included messages from both Queen Victoria and the Khedive.

The next morning, Friday 13 September, was not an unlucky one for the obelisk, for it was gently lowered the few inches onto its pedestal without any complications. After careful checks had been carried out to verify that it was truly vertical, it was then firmly settled in place by a final push from the hydraulic jacks. Within a few days the wrought iron jacket had been removed, and work begun dismantling the now redundant wooden framework. Early in October the last of the heavy timbers was lowered into a waiting boat giving the public an unimpeded view of the Cleopatra's Needle in its new setting.

7

The American Needle

No sooner had the prostrate Cleopatra's Needle been unearthed and safely cocooned in the *Cleopatra*, than plans were being drawn up in New York concerning the fate of its twin companion which still stood erect on the Alexandrian foreshore. Over the years suggestions had been made by some of her citizens that the United States of America should follow the example set by the French and acquire an obelisk to adorn one of her principal cities. In 1869 when visiting Egypt to attend the opening ceremony of the Suez Canal, the editor of the *New York World*, William Hurlbert, discussed the matter with Khedive Ismail Pasha—but nothing concrete resulted. There the matter rested until the summer of 1877 when Hurlbert's interest in the project was re-awakened by the news reports coming out of Egypt. These made it clear that the British really were in earnest this time about claiming their Cleopatra's Needle, and now that the Londoners could at long last look forward to the happy prospect of having an obelisk of their very own, Hurlbert was determined that New York should be similarly blessed. Through an intermediary he was put in touch with John Dixon, and negotiations were entered into by telegraph in September 1877 over the cost of transporting the remaining Cleopatra's Needle to America, and it quickly transpired that Dixon was willing to consider undertaking the commission for the sum of £15,000. Hurlbert then contacted Henry Stebbins, the Commissioner of Public Parks for the City of New York, and Stebbins agreed both to provide a suitable site for the obelisk and to try and raise money privately to finance the project. He approached the multi-millionaire railroad king William Vanderbilt and asked him to head a subscription list. Luckily the idea of erecting an Egyptian obelisk in America's leading city so captivated Vanderbilt's imagination that he enthusiastically offered to foot the entire bill.

So far so good, but a diplomatic approach was obviously going to be needed to persuade the Egyptian Government to part with the needle, so on 15 October the assistance of the State Department was sought. The Secretary of State, William Evarts, immediately agreed to throw the full weight of his department behind the venture, and four days later he instructed his Consul-General in Cairo to open negotiations with the Khedive. Six weeks later the State Department received a letter from its Egyptian representative Elbert Farman, informing them that he feared 'there will be serious opposition to the removal of the obelisk from the city of Alexandria, so much in fact, that although the Khedive might personally desire to gratify the wishes of the citizens of New York, he would not think it best to grant their request.'[1] When Farman put the proposal to Ismail Pasha, the Khedive seemed surprised at the idea, but after some discussion he agreed to consider the possibility of presenting a different obelisk to America. The matter was raised again by Farman on several subsequent occasions, and finally the Khedive instructed one of his

50 The American needle. A view of the obelisk at Alexandria shortly before it was removed and taken to New York by Lieutenant-Commander Gorringe.(From *L'Egypt* by G. Ebers).

ministers to prepare a report on the subject. Shortly afterwards at a diplomatic reception Farman met the minister concerned, Brugsch Bey, and the following conversation ensued:

"I learn you are trying to obtain an obelisk to take to New York."

"Why not? They have one in Paris and one in London, and the people of New York wish one also."

"You will create a great amount of feeling; all the scholars of Europe will oppose it. The Khedive has asked me to give a description of the obelisks remaining in Egypt, and to state which one can best be spared; I have sent a description of the obelisks, but I shall not designate any to be taken away, for I am totally opposed to the removal of any of them."[2]

Inevitably the news leaked out, and strong disapproval was voiced to the American proposals, not merely by Egyptians and foreigners residing in Egypt, but also by prominent men in other countries. Some Americans also deplored the very idea of plundering Egypt of one of its obelisks, and petitions were drawn up opposing the plan. One petition signed by the Governor of Rhode Island did not mince words and stated that 'violating a reverence for antiquity would misrepresent the American people and be an act of vandalism which must ultimately receive the scorn of the civilised world.'[3] With regard to the Cleopatra's Needle most of the opposition believed that it was one thing to remove an unwanted and half forgotten obelisk which had lain buried in the sand for centuries, but quite a different kettle of fish to pull down a local landmark of such great historical interest and cart it away.

However, if the remaining Cleopatra's Needle was left where it was on the edge of the Mediterranean, its safety would be seriously jeopardised. In May 1877 Waynman Dixon had excavated around its base and he discovered that two of the four bronze crabs used by the Romans to support the obelisk had been stolen, and that the equilibrium of the needle was only precariously maintained by rough stones crudely wedged into position. The following October Dixon addressed a meeting of the British Archaeological Association and warned them:

The standing obelisk was found to be in a very dangerous condition. It is 12ins. out of the perpendicular, and inclined towards the sea, which is every year encroaching rapidly on the ground on which it stands. A serious crack, too, exists in the base of the obelisk, on the side towards which it leans. A succinct report on this perilous condition of one of Egypt's most interesting historic monuments was . . . personally presented by myself to the Khedive, who expressed much interest in it, and ordered that the proposed steps should be taken to render it temporarily secure, at an estimated expense of £100 to £200; but the obstructiveness and cupidity of engineers of the fortifications have frustrated its execution, and it is to be feared that the standing obelisk will shortly share the fate of its prostrate companion so lately removed.[4]

Farman persisted gently in his overtures, and in May 1879 was pleased to learn from the Egyptian Minister of Foreign Affairs that the Khedive had decided to present the Alexandrian obelisk to America. The exact reason for his change of mind is not certain, but is believed to have been prompted by his precarious political position. In recent years a war with Abyssinia, trouble in the Sudan, and bad harvests, had stretched the resources of the Egyptian Government to breaking point. Unable to pay foreign debts they had been forced to accept representatives of the main creditors, Britain and France, in key positions within the Egyptian Cabinet, and Ismail Pasha had been partially stripped of his powers. Then, in April 1879 a coup d'état resulted in the dismissal of the European ministers, and a month later the Khedive presented the obelisk to the City of New York. Possibly he wished to demonstrate his independence, for the main objectors to the removal of the needle were European. At any rate within two months Anglo-French pressure led to his downfall and he was deposed in favour of his eldest son Tewfik, and Ismail Pasha went into exile. He died at Constantinople in 1895. Bearing in mind that Britain had waited over fifty years before collecting her gift, perhaps when the Khedive succumbed to American pressure he hoped they would be in no hurry to remove the remaining Cleopatra's Needle. If this is so, his optimism was almost as short lived as his reign, for the Americans soon showed that they did not believe in letting the grass grow under their feet.

On receipt of the good news Hurlbert immediately contacted John Dixon, who, in light of the troubles he had since experienced with the British needle, raised the price at which he would be prepared to undertake the task of transporting its twin across the Atlantic from £15,000 to £20,000. Hurlbert was annoyed, and without even bothering to consult Vanderbilt he declined Dixon's offer and issued an appeal to his fellow countrymen for

51 Henry Honeychurch Gorringe, (1841-85). This portrait was engraved from a photograph taken around 1881.(*The Century Magazine,* 1882).

help. In the short space of six weeks various proposals were submitted, considered, and rejected, before a plan of action drawn up by Lieutenant-Commander Henry Gorringe of the US Navy was approved at the beginning of August 1879. An agreement was soon drawn up and signed under which Gorringe was to receive 75,000 dollars (£15,500) from William Vanderbilt if he succeeded in erecting the obelisk in New York. As with the bargain struck between John Dixon and Erasmus Wilson, the contract was very much of a gamble for neither was the exact site finalised, nor would the unfortunate contractor be entitled to receive any payment whatsoever if he failed to complete his mission.

Henry Honeychurch Gorringe was born in Barbados in August 1841, the son of an English clergyman who held the rectorship at Tobago. By the time he was twenty years old young Henry had settled in the USA, where during the Civil War he joined the navy and received a commendation for bravery after the gunboat he commanded, the *Cricket*, was severely damaged in an action fought in April 1864 on the Red River. As soon as Gorringe's plan was accepted the United States Navy readily gave leave of absence to both Gorringe and a fellow officer, Lieutenant Seaton Schroeder, who was to assist him. Gorringe had studied carefully the methods adopted by LeBas and Dixon, and after extracting certain features which he considered suitable he rejected the rest. Dixon had wrapped a pivoting jacket around the middle of his needle and had then supported it on a turning cradle when swinging it into a vertical position on the Thames Embankment. Gorringe fully approved of this idea, and decided to use it both for the lowering of his 'obelisk at Alexandria and for its subsequent erection again in New York. In August 1879 he placed the order for this equipment and other items including a transporting cradle with one of America's leading engineering companies, Roeblings of Trenton, New Jersey.

Throughout the whole operation Gorringe was to be continually faced with difficulties and obstructions, and it was only his dogged persistence and mechanical ingenuity which were to enable him to see the job through to a successful conclusion. He appears to have had a fairly complex character. Schroeder, by then an admiral, commented many years later that Gorringe had unlimited self-confidence, but unfortunately at times reacted rather sensitively to views expressed by other people, and he seems to have had the knack of rubbing them the wrong way. His first difficulty was procuring sufficient funds to carry out the undertaking, since the contract only provided for payment on completion. The banks were not interested in risks of this magnitude, and finally a friend, who obviously had a great deal of faith in the ability of Gorringe, came to the rescue with a loan. For three weeks Gorringe tried unsuccessfully to charter an American steamer to transport the needle from Alexandria, then sailed for England at the end of August 1879. At Liverpool he spent a further two weeks trying to find a British shipowner who would be prepared to undertake the task. After hearing details of the cargo and the way in which Gorringe intended loading it, most shipowners were not only sceptical of the chances of success, but, concerned for the safety of their ships, were not prepared to touch the job under any circumstances. The only terms he could obtain were so high that he decided it would be cheaper to wait until he reached Alexandria, buy a secondhand steamer and organise the shipping himself.

In mid-October Gorringe at last set foot in Alexandria to be met by a torrent of protests, abuse, and even threats of personal violence, if he should so much as dare even to touch the remaining Cleopatra's Needle. By now the Egyptian Government was being strongly petitioned to change its mind over presenting the obelisk to New York, for as yet it had not been formally handed over. Gorringe travelled to Cairo, and accompanied by Consul-General Farman was granted an audience with the new Khedive, Tewfik, who agreed to honour the promise made by his father, and a few days later the Cleopatra's Needle officially became American property. The efforts of the protesters were now concentrated on preventing its removal, and as soon as the first labourers moved onto the site they were ordered off by an Italian who falsely claimed that the land belonged to him. To bolster his claim he had erected a shanty next to the needle, and threatened to use force of arms if necessary to evict trespassers. At first Gorringe tried a peaceful approach and offered to rent the ground for the duration of the removal operation, but when this met with a point-blank refusal he passed the buck to the Egyptian Government informing them that if they were unable to resolve the matter quickly 'I shall be compelled to telegraph to my government that I have been forcibly ejected, and that Egyptian authority has failed to protect me.'[5] This piece of gun-boat diplomacy worked like magic, for within hours the affair had been resolved, and early the next morning, 29 October, the work began in earnest.

The first job was to excavate the base of the obelisk to examine its condition and then to prepare the foundations for the apparatus which would be used to lower it to the ground. Within a week the needle had been surrounded from top to bottom by temporary staging which provided a series of working platforms from which joiners then assembled a made-to-measure packing case around the obelisk to protect it in transit. The items ordered from Roeblings in New Jersey had arrived and soon the special jacket complete with trunnions was strapped around the middle of the needle. By 2 December the steel supporting towers were in place and all was ready for the lifting operation to begin.

While all this activity was going on the opposition had not been idle. Someone had persuaded a disgruntled creditor of the Egyptian Government to try and further his case by applying to the courts for a writ to prevent the obelisk being moved pending settlement of the claim. Since the obelisk was no longer Egyptian property the courts had no alternative but to reject the application. To discourage further harassment and to emphasise American ownership, the United States flag was flown from the top of the obelisk and guards were posted to deter would-be intruders. Foreign archaeologists residing in Egypt then banded together and persuaded their consul-generals to remind the Egyptian Government of its obligations under a convention entered into some years previously which banned the export of antiquities. The legal validity of the convention was open to question, and in any case it had often been flouted in the past—for instance when the British needle was removed—and while the matter was under consideration Gorringe pushed ahead as fast as he could working his men day and night.

On 3 December the obelisk was lifted off its granite base and its whole weight was taken by the trunnions and their supporting towers. The trunnion jacket had on purpose been fitted about ten inches below the centre of gravity of the needle, making it slightly top heavy, to facilitate swinging it into a horizontal position. Meanwhile in order to keep it vertical while the 50 ton pedestal and the bronze crabs were removed, workmen had attached steadying cables to the top and bottom of the obelisk. It was rumoured that foreign residents and other protesters were planning to stage a demonstration as the critical operation of turning the needle into the horizontal position took place. As he made his final inspection of the arrangements on the morning of 6 December Gorringe was heartened by the sight of a cordon of unarmed Russian sailors who effectively kept the

public at bay. Rear-Admiral Aslambekoff of the Russian Imperial Navy was currently paying a courtesy call to Alexandria in his flagship *Minim,* and on hearing the rumours had, without waiting to be asked, responded in the true maritime tradition and come to the aid of a fellow mariner. By mid-morning all the vantage points around the obelisk were occupied by a noisy crowd of spectators, who, when the massive needle slowly started to turn were reduced to a respectful silence. As the top of the needle slowly inched downwards, like the minute hand of a clock, the creaking of the ropes and pulley blocks could be clearly heard. Suddenly, when the obelisk had completed half of its journey, the movement was arrested throwing such a strain onto the two ropes that one of them parted with a loud snap. The man controlling the other tried in vain to check the movement of the obelisk, but then his rope also failed. As the workmen fled for their lives the huge monolith continued its downward swing and with a resounding crash struck the top of a timber staging which had been strategically placed for such an eventuality. The staging was reduced in height by several feet due to the impact, but although the cast iron jacket split the needle was undamaged. When the scurrying workmen stopped and looked back, they and everyone else connected with the project were at first surprised, and then pleased, by a burst of cheering from the spectators. It was, as Gorringe later said 'the first friendly manifestation shown by the Alexandrians.'[6]

The next stage of the operation was to lower the horizontal needle, and here Gorringe used in reverse Dixon's system for raising his obelisk on the Thames Embankment. The weight of the horizontal beam was taken by two stacks of timber, one at each end, and after the trunnions and supporting towers had been dismantled, the obelisk was lowered in stages using hydraulic jacks. Originally it had been Gorringe's intention to lower it directly onto a transporting cradle and then to haul it just under a mile through the streets of Alexandria to the dry-dock for loading aboard a steamer. However, the opposition again showed its hand. Foreign merchants residing locally demonstrated the influence they had with the Governor of Alexandria by persuading him to ban the obelisk from the streets on the grounds that its weight would damage the sewers. Gorringe offered to sign guarantees for the repair of any damage caused, but to no avail, and he was compelled to follow Dixon's example and get his needle to the dry-dock by sea. This entailed building a wooden caisson, an open topped box, large enough to contain the obelisk and strong enough to act as a barge for the ten mile sea journey round the headland. Constructing the caisson was a simple task costing a mere 2,200 dollars, but the expense of getting it afloat eventually cost Gorringe about ten times as much. It was necessary to launch the caisson into fairly deep water, and to this end over four months were spent on the construction of a launching slip which when it was eventually completed stretched out over one hundred yards beyond the low water mark. The final stages of this operation were carried out in March, the stormiest month of the year, and time and again a storm would in a matter of hours destroy several days work. Finally, on 18 March 1880, the caisson containing its precious cargo stood at the top of the launching way which sloped down into the choppy water with an inclination of 1 in 15. Off-shore a tug lay waiting to tow the caisson round to

Opposite
52 Turning the obelisk. The scene at Alexandria on 6 December 1879 as the American needle was being swung into the horizontal position by Henry Gorringe. The building in the background is presumably that being erected by Demetrio on the site previously occupied by the London needle.(From *Egyptian Obelisks* by H. H. Gorringe).

53 The American needle horizontal. During the turning operation in December 1879 both control ropes snapped and the needle's downward plunge was arrested by a strategically placed pile of timber which was reduced in height by several feet due to the impact.(From *Egyptian Obelisks* by H. H. Gorringe).

the harbour. At 11.00am the order was given to release the caisson and it began its journey down to the sea. After sliding freely for twenty feet under its own volition it suddenly ground to a halt, and refused to budge even when attached by a tow line to the tug. At first Gorringe thought that the setback would be of short duration, but as Waynman Dixon had recently discovered obelisks seem reluctant to take the plunge. It took two weeks hard work before hydraulic rams finally managed to persuade the caisson to move all the way. It eventually took to the water on 31 March, and its reluctance was soon shown to be unwarranted, for five hours later the caisson was safely moored in the harbour at Alexandria.

As soon as work had started on the removal of the obelisk at the end of October 1879, Gorringe began to search for a suitable steamer to purchase for the voyage to New York. For once Lady Luck was on his side, for almost immediately he discovered the *Dessoug* lying at Alexandria. An inspection soon showed that she suited his needs admirably. The main requirements were that the vessel should have a forehold long enough to take the crated needle, that there should be sufficient clearance between the floor of the hold and the overhead deck beams, and that her bows should not be too finely shaped. On the debit side, although her hull was structurally sound, the steam engines and boilers of this fifteen year old vessel were in a very bad condition. After protracted negotiations Gorringe

100

54 Embarking the pedestal. The pedestal was a granite block weighing 50 tons. Since lifting it was beyond the capability of the dockside crane, the job of loading the pedestal into the rear hold of the *Dessoug* was shared by a floating crane. As the pedestal was being manoeuvred one of the four steel cables supporting it failed, but luckily the huge stone did not fall or the *Dessoug*'s fate would have been sealed. The loading was carried out successfully on 6 March 1880.(From *Egyptian Obelisks* by H. H. Gorringe).

purchased her in December 1879 for £5,100. Lieutenant Schroeder was placed in charge of repairing and refitting the *Dessoug*, which was destined to bring the total cost of the steamer up to nearly £10,000, while Gorringe concentrated his attention on the obelisk itself. To prevent any possibility of interference Schroeder posted guards on the gangways and the Stars and Stripes was flown at each masthead.

By the beginning of May 1880 the repairs to the *Dessoug* had been completed and on 10 May she was admitted to the dry-dock where the crated obelisk awaited her. Due to its weight and length it was pointless to even consider lifting the needle on board, let alone trying to lower it into the hold, and Gorringe's plan of action consisted of cutting a hole in the bow of the *Dessoug* and sliding the obelisk in. Certain alterations had already been made to the vessel, the most important of which consisted of strengthening the floor of the forehold with steel beams and covering them with a timber deck. The hole in the bow was to be cut on the starboard side below the waterline, and as this entailed not only removing plates, but also cutting away parts of frames, a foreman shipwright had been imported especially from Glasgow to superintend the work. As soon as the water had been pumped out of the dry-dock, three gangs of Arab boilermakers began working shifts around the clock to produce a large enough aperture, while teams of carpenters began laying a timber staging from the obelisk to the *Dessoug* to support a steel track along which the obelisk could be rolled on cannon balls. Ten days after she entered the dock everything was ready and within hours the crated needle had been smoothly slid into the hold. Another ten days were needed to replace the frames and plates, to align the obelisk fore and aft above the keel of the ship, and to wedge it so securely in place that not even the severest of storms was likely to move it—a precaution taken as much for the safety of the *Dessoug* as for the benefit of her precious cargo—before the vessel was refloated on 1 June.

Gorringe and Schroeder now found themselves in something of a quandary, for as professional naval officers they were faced with an embarrassing decision. Under American law the *Dessoug* could not be registered in the United States, and Egyptian registration was out of the question as it would have opened the door for court action to be taken by those who wished to prevent the Cleopatra's Needle leaving Egypt. To Gorringe the thought of flying a British flag, or even that of some other European country, was objectionable, and in the end he decided that there was no alternative but to defy maritime law and sail without the protection of a flag, and risk having his vessel seized, either at any port they entered, or even on the high seas by a man-of-war. Manning the *Dessoug* also proved a headache, and in the end Gorringe had to make do with British officers and engineers and a crew from Trieste. He obviously held most of them in very low esteem, for he later wrote:

The first and second officers turned out to be confirmed drunkards; the latter so bad that he had to be dismissed to prevent him from killing himself. He fell twice from the second deck into the hold, and twice overboard, while drunk. The engineers were useful, hard-working, hard-drinking men. The quartermasters would do credit to a pirate's crew. The number of men who solemnly enlisted for the voyage and speedily deserted before it began, was forty-eight.[7]

Eventually, after coaling and taking on supplies, the *Dessoug* was able to cast off and steam out of Alexandria on the afternoon of 12 June 1880. As she headed west Lieutenant-Commander Gorringe and Lieutenant Schroeder at last found themselves back in an environment which was not only familiar, but enjoyable after the long frustrating months in Alexandria. The weight of the obelisk in the forehold had been counteracted in the aft hold by that of the trunnions, steel supporting towers and other equipment which would be needed to re-erect the needle, plus its steps and pedestal, and sufficient ballast to trim the ship. The *Dessoug* soon proved a good sea-boat, and Gorringe noted with satisfaction that the pitching and rolling motions of his ship were slow and gentle. Despite several days of headwinds, some violent squalls and a gale, she made good progress and reached Gibraltar at the other end of the Mediterranean on 22 June, having averaged 7 knots. So far Gorringe had avoided calling at any port, but now he needed to replenish his coal bunkers for the Atlantic crossing. Although the *Dessoug* carried a fair spread of sail, Gorringe did not want to have to rely on the vagaries of the wind; so gambling on the personal contacts he had made a few years previously with the authorities at Gibraltar, he decided to put into port for coal and risk having his vessel seized. Lord Napier, the

Governor of Gibraltar, not only followed the Nelson tradition by turning a blind eye to the lack of registration, but accompanied by his wife and staff honoured the *Dessoug* with a formal visit to see the obelisk.

After taking on over five hundred tons of coal the ship slipped her moorings at midnight on 25 June and sailed out into the Atlantic. Five days later having experienced some variable weather with heavy seas she passed the Azores. Another week saw her in mid-Atlantic steaming steadily westward in calm weather, when suddenly after a short period of running erratically the engines ground to a stop. The cause was not difficult to find, for the after-crank shaft had snapped. Fortunately there were some spare sections of shafting on board, but it took six days of non-stop activity to effect the repairs. During this anxious time the weather was mostly fine with light winds, except for one day when it was very squally. On several occasions water spouts were seen, and one greatly alarmed Gorringe by coming within fifty yards of his defenceless ship before veering away to disintegrate harmlessly at a safe distance. The repairs were completed on 12 July and better progress was then made under steam until a severe south-west gale struck. The *Dessoug* took a battering as the wind whipped up heavy seas. Some of these were shipped damaging the boats and skylights, but the obelisk had been so securely shored that despite the vessel rolling and pitching quite heavily, her cargo did not budge. She steamed into New York Bay on 19 July 1880 and after lying overnight at the Quarantine Station on Staten Island received clearance to move up river. The *Dessoug* then entered the Hudson and moored off Twenty-third Street.

Like the Londoners the citizens of New York held varying opinions as to where their Cleopatra's Needle should stand. Most of the sites suggested were at junctions of busy streets, but Gorringe and the promotors of the venture, newspaper editor William Hurlbert and millionaire William Vanderbilt, all favoured Graywacke Knoll in Central Park. Here the obelisk would be able to stand in splendid isolation away from tall buildings and the hustle and bustle of daily life, and yet still be easily accessible to the public. The Commissioner of Public Parks, Henry Stebbins, had been involved in the project right from the start, and when he put the idea before his Board in May 1880 they unanimously approved of Graywacke Knoll. The Board also approved the placing of a collection of contemporary objects in the obelisk's foundations, and when requesting suitable material Gorringe surprisingly received many rebuffs, possibly due to his rather abrasive manner. He unsuccessfully tried to obtain an example of the wonder of the age—a telephone, and when he asked the American Bible Society to contribute a copy of the New Testament, they apparently suggested he bought one—so he did. An application for copies of the standard weights and measures was also turned down. Other government departments were more helpful, and some even provided copies of current reports hermetically sealed in copper containers which in turn were cased in lead. Other items interred in the foundations included the works of William Shakespeare and a hydraulic jack of the type used to lower the needle at Alexandria. The corner stone was laid at a ceremony held on 9 October, and nearly nine thousand Freemasons marched in parade through the streets of New York to attend.

As soon as he arrived in New York Gorringe began making arrangements for disembarking the obelisk and transporting it to Central Park. Initially he intended putting the loading plan into reverse. Unfortunately, realising the strong position they were in, the owners of the only suitable dry-dock available not only tried to charge an exorbitant fee,

56 Crossing the Hudson River Railroad. The Cleopatra's Needle being hauled across the railroad tracks at the foot of New York's Ninety-sixth Street on 25 September 1880.(From *Egyptian Obelisks* by H. H. Gorringe).

but insisted on conditions which Gorringe refused to entertain. Due to the size of the obelisk the only feasible alternative was to use one of the local marine railways, a system by which a vessel that had been floated into a cradle could be hauled on rollers up an incline and out of the water. Gorringe duly made the necessary arrangements with a firm on Staten Island and on 21 August the unprotesting *Dessoug* was left high and dry. Three weeks later after a special disembarking stage had been erected on temporary piles driven into the sea-bed, all was ready for the crated needle to emerge from the gaping aperture which had been re-opened in the bow of the vessel. The operation went so smoothly that within an hour the obelisk had been extracted as easily as a loose tooth and lay in its wooden case on the staging. The next job was to ferry it by water as close as possible to its destination, so Gorringe strapped a pair of pontoons side by side, and at low tide manoeuvred them into position beneath the staging. They rose with the incoming tide taking the obelisk with them, and a waiting tug quickly towed the pontoons twelve miles on the flood tide across New York Harbour and up the River Hudson. Within a matter of hours the fastly ebbing water had deposited the pontoons on to another specially constructed landing stage at the foot of Ninety-sixth Street on Manhatten Island.

The needle had now reached the start of the last phase of its travels from Alexandria—the two mile journey through the streets of New York to Central Park. First of all an obstacle had to be crossed, for the main line of the Hudson River Railroad ran along the river bank cutting the obelisk off from the road. Anything other than a brief interruption to scheduled train services would obviously be unacceptable, so under Gorringe's direction the parts of a temporary crossing were pre-fabricated and preparations were made to haul the needle over the crossing by means of a cable wound around the rotating drum of a steam-driven pile driver. The trains continued to run normally until the morning of 25 September, when at the appointed time gangs of men sprang into action. In little over an hour the operation had been successfully completed and the temporary crossing dismantled again, and only the passage of a solitary freight train had been impeded.

The route to Graywacke Knoll had been selected with a view to minimising gradients and using the widest streets. It consisted of ascending Ninety-sixth Street, turning right into West Boulevard then left at Eighty-sisth Street, at the eastern end of which the obelisk was to enter Central Park. However, to reach Graywacke Knoll it was deemed best to completely traverse the park from west to east, and then to proceed three blocks down Fifth Avenue before re-entering the park. The final 900 feet lay over rough open ground and the entire crossing was to be made on a purpose built trestle bridge. The journey through the streets was accomplished as follows: The obelisk was carried on a cradle which was moved on rollers along lengths of marine railway track. These were successively laid down in front of the cradle and taken up again after it had passed. The power was provided by a pile-driver engine mounted on the front of the cradle. The engine wound in the tow-rope, the other end of which was also fastened to the front of the cradle, and since the rope also passed around a pulley securely fixed to the road some distance ahead, the vehicle was able to haul itself along. Thus the journey was made in a series of traverses and in general it proceeded fairly smoothly. On the best day a straight run of nearly 600 feet was achieved, but the daily average for the two mile journey was under 100 feet. Extra care was needed on gradients and teams of men were ready with wedges to place beneath the rollers if a braking effect was needed. Rounding street corners took time and the weather also caused some delays, for that Autumn had more than its fair share of heavy snow showers and cold snaps. Eventually on 5 January 1881 the Cleopatra's Needle arrived at its new home.

The Egyptians had mounted their obelisks directly onto the stone pedestals, but the Romans had favoured four metal crabs—one at each corner. Due to the worn nature of the needle's base Gorringe decided to use both methods to ensure stability, and four bronze supports were cast, each individually shaped to fit its own corner. Between them they weighed one and a half tons. Within ten days of its arrival in Central Park the transporting cradle had been dismantled and the obelisk was supported in a horizontal position high in the air above the pedestal by the steel towers and trunnions used twelve months earlier at Alexandria. All was now ready for the final operation which was scheduled for noon on 22

Opposite
57 Erecting the American Needle. The scene in Central Park on a cold snowy day in January 1881. Gorringe used the same simple steel framework previously employed at Alexandria—a system which proved equally as effective as the massive timber structure chosen by Dixon for erecting the London obelisk.(From *Egyptian Obelisks* by H. H. Gorringe).

106

58 Central Park. The Cleopatra's Needle standing in its stark simplicity on Graywacke Knoll contrasts strongly with its former companion in London (See Figures 62 and 63) which has been heavily embellished by the addition of bronze plaques, ornamental castings, and two enormous sphinxes. The American obelisk is somewhat the larger of the two, standing 69ft 6ins high and weighing 200 tons, it is twelve inches taller and fourteen tons heavier than the London needle.

January. The day dawned to a wintry scene: a thick carpet of snow covered the ground and there was a bitterly cold wind. Even so an estimated 10,000 people turned out to witness the final act, and the US Navy had obliged with a guard of honour and a Marine band. Shortly before noon editor William Hurlbert, Secretary of State Evarts, and other distinguished guests took their seats on the platform. On a hand signal from Lieutenant-Commander Gorringe the obelisk began to move. Five minutes later it had turned the full 90⁰, and as it reached the vertical the previously hushed crowd spontaneously burst into applause. The band struck up, the guard of honour presented arms, and a delighted Gorringe no doubt heaved a sigh of relief since everything had gone without a hitch. Because of the cold weather the crowd quickly dispersed and few people were around when the obelisk was gently lowered into position. With its full weight taken by the crabs and pedestal the now redundant jacket, trunnions, and towers, were again removed leaving the Cleopatra's Needle standing erect, and alone, in its new setting.

One more rite remained—the official presentation to the City of New York. In view of the season it was held indoors, the venue appropriately being the nearby Metropolitan Museum. Inevitably the ceremony followed the usual pattern, for the length of the speeches more than compensated for the lack of them at Graywacke Knoll on that bitterly cold day one month earlier.

8

Postscript

Probably the most bizarre part of this story concerns the fate of the *Dessoug*. Once she had fulfilled her role of carrying the obelisk to New York, Gorringe decided to sell her. Being foreign built, under United States law she was not permitted to fly the Stars and Stripes, and she had in fact entered American territorial waters illegally without the protection of either nationality or registration. Naturally the Americans were proud of Gorringe's achievement, and it was strongly felt in some quarters that after rendering such sterling service for the United States that the *Dessoug* should not be allowed to fall into foreign hands. Several petitions on the subject were drawn up by responsible bodies and presented to the government, with the result that a special act was drafted. After being quickly passed by both the Congress and Senate it was signed by the President on 8 February 1881. The act honoured the *Dessoug* by granting her American registration, and she was subsequently bought by the Ocean Steamship Company of Savannah.

When the needle arrived in New York in July 1880 Gorringe was desperately short of money, so Vanderbilt advanced part of the agreed 75,000 dollars to enable him to complete the contract. The cause of the trouble was the unexpectedly high expenditure at Alexandria, and eventually the project overran its budget to cost just over 100,000 dollars. At the contemporary rate of exchange this was about £1,000 more than the fee demanded by John Dixon. Vanderbilt generously met the full bill, and after paying all the debts he had incurred Gorringe was left with a net profit of 1,150 dollars—a meagre sum, but much better than the huge loss sustained by John Dixon over the London needle. In 1882 Gorringe resigned from the US Navy after being severely criticised over public statements he had made on naval policy, and tragically he died three years later from spinal injuries received in a fall from a train.

The day before the *Cleopatra* left Alexandria John Dixon took out insurance cover for the voyage with two firms of London underwriters, a precaution which soon appeared to have been a wise move. After the action for salvage costs had been settled in the Admiralty Court he submitted a claim on his insurance policies and was, to put it mildly, surprised when the underwriters disclaimed any liability. Subsequently a very disgruntled Dixon sued them and the case was heard in the Court of Common Pleas in April 1879. The underwriters pleaded that their policies were for total loss only, and patently this had not been the case since the vessel and its cargo had been returned to its owner. The court agreed with this point of view, but even so gave judgement in Dixon's favour. It was ruled that the underwriters were the beneficiaries of the salvage operation, for it was solely due to the action of the *Fitzmaurice* that the *Cleopatra* was saved from becoming a total loss. Therefore they must pay the £2,000 awarded in salvage. Curiously the court also ruled that

AT LAST!

59 The Hero. A *Punch* cartoon depicting the hero of the lifting operation on the Thames Embankment—Hydraulic Jack, telling everyone 'I did it'. Thanks to the availability of hydraulic power both Dixon and Gorringe employed far less manpower than Fontana and LeBas had found necessary when erecting their obelisks in Rome and Paris.(*Punch* 1878).

the underwriters were not liable for the legal costs incurred by Dixon in the Admiralty Court when he succeeded in reducing Burrell's salvage claim from £5,000 down to £2,000, even though it was the underwriters who obviously benefitted. Such are the quirks of the English legal system.

The Court of Common Pleas had barely finished pronouncing its strange verdict when the House of Lords reversed the judgement given in another maritime insurance case, which had the effect of altering the previously held interpretation of the law as regards a crucial phrase in Dixon's insurance policies. Ten months later, in March 1880, the Court of Appeal upset the decision given in Dixon's favour, and John Dixon was unfortunately saddled with the burden of paying not only the salvage award and his own legal costs, but also those of his opponents in all three cases. In October 1878 he had received the promised £10,000 from Erasmus Wilson, and this had just covered the basic cost of the whole operation. However, Dixon was eventually out of pocket to the tune of a further £10,000, for the abandonment of the *Cleopatra* in the Bay of Biscay cost him dear. To the salvage award of £2,000 must be added a further £1,500 for the associated legal fees, plus some £5,000 for the two court actions involving the insurers of the *Cleopatra*, together with the extra expenses involved in refitting her at Ferrol and towing her to London. The only winners in this sorry series of legal battles were the owners of the *Fitzmaurice*, her crew who earned their money the hard way, and the legal profession whose fees amounted to over £6,000. As one journal put it, in future, 'however anxious people may be to preserve for the nation such ancient monuments, most would pause before incurring like responsibilities.'[1]

As soon as the Cleopatra's Needle took up residence on the Thames Embankment the press began to speculate on whether or not official recognition would, or indeed should, be bestowed upon the men responsible. It was felt in some circles that Erasmus Wilson had the best claim to a knighthood, since he had provided the financial incentive which led to London being graced by the presence of an Egyptian obelisk. Another much harsher view was that he had backed a certain winner, for if the venture had failed it would have cost him nothing, but its success, bought for a paltry £10,000, had assured him of great public acclaim and the near certainty of a knighthood. John Dixon's prospects were less promising, for as the contractor who had carried out the scheme he had, in theory at any rate, stood a chance of making a profit, although his 'no cure, no pay' contract and the novelty of the project had made a financial loss the more likely outcome. *The Engineer* commented rather unfairly that he 'did the work well, no doubt, but he lost money in his contract. It was the purest matter of business with him, and certainly honours will be cheap in this country if loss in business is to be a good reason for their concession.'[2] And what about General Alexander? Surely he should receive some recognition, for it was thanks to his ceaseless efforts that the plan to bring the needle to Britain had eventually got off the ground. In the event Wilson was the only one to be honoured by his country. He was knighted by Queen Victoria at Windsor Castle in December 1881, an honour which not only recognised the importance of the role he had played in bringing the Cleopatra's Needle to London, but also his munificence in endowing various medical charities. Sir William James Erasmus Wilson died soon afterwards in August 1884, and eight months later General Alexander also departed from the scene. Of the engineers concerned John Dixon passed away at the comparatively early age of 56 years in 1891, but his younger brother Waynman outlived him by nearly fifty years, while Benjamin Baker had at the time of his death in 1907 become one of Britain's most celebrated engineers.

During the construction of the obelisk's pedestal John Dixon sealed within it two large earthenware jars containing a collection of contemporary objects. Perhaps, at some time in the distant future an archaeologist will excavate the site and find these relics of a former half-forgotten civilisation. They formed a rather miscellaneous assortment, comprising

Standard foot and pound, presented by the standard department of the Board of Trade; bronze model of the obelisk, ½inch scale to the foot, cast and presented by Mr. Joseph Whitley, of Leeds; copies of *Engineering*, printed on vellum, with plans of the various arrangements and details employed in erecting and transporting the obelisk, together with its complete history, presented by the proprietors of the publication; jars of Doulton ware, presented by Doulton and Co.; a piece of the obelisk stone; complete set of British coinage, including an Empress of India rupee [Victoria adopted this title in 1877]; parchment copy of Dr. Birch's translation of the obelisk's hieroglyphics; standard gauge to 1000th part of an inch as sample of accurate workmanship, presented by J. Holtzapffel; portrait of her Majesty the Queen; bibles in various languages, presented by the British and Foreign Bible Society; Bradshaw's railway guide; Mappin's shilling razor, case of cigars, pipes, box of hairpins and sundry articles of female adornment; Alexandra feeding-bottle and children's toys, presented by a lady; a Tangye's hydraulic jack as used in raising the obelisk, presented by Tangye Brothers; wire ropes and specimens of submarine cables, presented by Mr. R. S. Newall; map of London, copies of the daily and illustrated papers; photographs of a dozen pretty Englishwomen, presented by Captain Henry Carter; a 2ft rule, a London Directory; *Whitaker's Almanack*, the last copy of the impression for the year, presented by the publishers.[3]

No doubt John Dixon, amongst others, was surprised when Captain Carter produced his contribution, but with all Carter had gone through who could refuse him? Shortly afterwards Henry Carter returned to his duties with the P & O, and regrettably he died in Bombay in January 1880 after a severe attack of dysentery.

The Metropolitan Board of Works decided to mount bronze plaques bearing a brief synopsis of the needle's history on the four faces of the pedestal. The names of Erasmus Wilson and John Dixon were to appear along with—apparently at the suggestion of Queen Victoria—those of the six brave seamen who perished in the vain rescue attempt in the Bay of Biscay. Dixon endeavoured to persuade the Board to add the names of the other men involved in the venture, however in February 1879 his request that the inscriptions should credit the part played by General Alexander, Giovanni Demetrio, Captain Carter, Waynman Dixon and Benjamin Baker, as well as several other people, was turned down. The four plaques tell the needle's story as follows:

East Side

West Side

| THIS OBELISK QUARRIED AT SYRENE
WAS ERECTED AT ON (HELIOPOLIS)
BY THE PHARAOH
THOTHMES III ABOUT 1500BC
LATERAL INSCRIPTIONS WERE ADDED
NEARLY TWO CENTURIES LATER
BY RAMESES THE GREAT.
REMOVED DURING THE GREEK DYNASTY
TO ALEXANDRIA
THE ROYAL CITY OF CLEOPATRA
IT WAS THERE ERECTED IN THE
18th YEAR OF AUGUSTUS CAESAR B.C. 12 | THIS OBELISK
PROSTRATE FOR CENTURIES
ON THE SANDS OF ALEXANDRIA
WAS PRESENTED TO THE
BRITISH NATION A.D.1819 BY
MAHOMMED ALI VICEROY OF EGYPT
A WORTHY MEMORIAL OF
OUR DISTINGUISHED COUNTRYMEN
NELSON AND ABERCROMBY. |

North Side

THROUGH THE PATRIOTIC ZEAL OF
ERASMUS WILSON F.R.S.
THIS OBELISK
WAS BROUGHT FROM ALEXANDRIA,
ENCASED IN AN IRON CYLINDER
IT WAS ABANDONED DURING A STORM
IN THE BAY OF BISCAY
RECOVERED AND ERECTED
ON THIS SPOT BY
JOHN DIXON C.E.
IN THE 42ND YEAR OF THE REIGN OF
QUEEN VICTORIA
1878

South Side

MICHAEL BURNS	WILLIAM ASKIN
WILLIAM DONALD	JAMES GARDINER
WILLIAM PATAN	JOSEPH BENBOW

PERISHED IN A BOLD ATTEMPT
TO SUCCOUR THE CREW OF THE
OBELISK SHIP "CLEOPATRA" DURING
THE STORM OCTOBER 14th 1877.

Although stonemasons had partly squared off the butt of the obelisk so as to enable it to stand in absolute safety on its pedestal, the broken and rounded corners still looked unsightly. Suggestions were made in the press that they should either be repaired or bronze crabs added, since the broken corners not only detracted from the appearance of the needle but created the impression that it was unstable. The Metropolitan Board of Works instructed their architect George Vulliamy to look into the matter, and he designed corner plates in the form of wings which were cast in bronze. These were linked together by four more castings bearing the cartouche, or insignia, of Pharaoh Thothmes III, so as to completely encircle the butt end of the Cleopatra's Needle.

On both the east and west sides of the platform where the needle had been erected was an existing stone plinth, and Vulliamy drew up plans for a huge sphinx to be mounted on each of them. His design was based upon a small black basalt sphinx bearing the cartouche of Thothmes III belonging to the Duke of Northumberland's collection of antiquities which is housed at Alnwick Castle. As a first step one was modelled full size in plaster, and after being coloured to look like bronze it was set up on one of the stone plinths in June 1880 so that the effect it produced could be gauged. Satisfied with the result the

60 The London needle. A view published immediately after Dixon erected it on the Embankment. The broken and rounded corners of the butt of the obelisk made it look unstable, and as is shown later these defects were soon hidden behind ornamental bronze castings.(*Engineering,* 1878).

Metropolitan Board of Works then ordered a pair of them to be cast in bronze at the nearby Eccleston Iron Works in Pimlico, not far from Victoria Station. On the morning of Saturday 19 March 1881 a large number of invited guests gathered at the foundry to witness the casting of the first sphinx from a bronze alloy consisting of nine parts of copper to one part of tin. Eight tons of metal had been heated in a cupola to 2,000°F and it was

61 Casting the Sphinx. The molten metal being poured into the mould at the Eccleston Iron Works, Pimlico, on Saturday 19 March 1881.(*The Illustrated London News,* 1881).

62 Cleopatra's Needle and Sphinxes. An artist's impression published shortly before the two sphinxes were placed upon their pedestals. At the last moment the decision was taken to mount them the other way round to face the obelisk.(*The Graphic,* 1881).

116

63 Cleopatra's Needle with the sphinxes the right way round. In the background is Hungerford Railway Bridge.

ceremoniously poured into the waiting mould just after midday. After fettling and polishing the finished casting weighed some seven tons, was 19ft long by 6ft wide, and 9ft high. A contemporary report describes it as the largest ornamental bronze casting yet produced, for although the lions surrounding Nelson's Column in Trafalgar Square are larger, they were each assembled from nineteen separate pieces. Initially it had been intended that the two sphinxes should crouch upon their plinths facing outwards, as though watchdogs entrusted with the task of keeping the public at bay, but at the last minute the plans were changed and instead they were positioned facing the needle so that they might study its hieroglyphics. The two sphinxes are reported to have cost £1,500, and by early February 1882 they and the other bronze embellishments had all been fixed in position.

Concern had been expressed that the smoky London atmosphere would not only begrime the hieroglyphics on the Cleopatra's Needle but prove injurious to the stone, so the Metropolitan Board of Works turned to its Chief Engineer and a consulting chemist for advice. As a result towards the end of April 1879 scaffolding was erected around the obelisk and workmen carefully cleaned off the thin layer of greasy soot which had already accumulated. The needle was then given two coats of Browning's Invisible Preservative. The work took a fortnight to complete, and it temporarily left the rose-red granite looking as fresh as when it had been unearthed from the sands of Egypt. In 1932 the London Fire Brigade turned their hoses on the by now heavily begrimed obelisk, and although this did not restore the monolith to its pristine condition, the pressure of the water jets dislodged plenty of dirt, and no doubt any loose pieces of stone. Since then the needle has been cleaned twice. In 1949 a detergent solution was used, but the results were not very long lasting, for in 1966 it was spring cleaned again—this time with the more delicate touch of compressed air—and it is to be hoped that with the advent of the Clean Air Act many years will elapse before the hieroglyphics are subjected to further treatment.

The Cleopatra's Needle has now stood on the Victoria Embankment for one hundred years, an honoured guest in an alien land with only the companionship of the sphinxes to remind it of the glories of the long extinct civilisation created by the ancient Egyptians. A century is but a brief chapter in its history, for nearly 3,500 years have elapsed since it was quarried from the red granite of Aswan at the command of the mighty warrior Pharaoh Thothmes III. Its story almost ended in September 1917, for it narrowly escaped destruction in a German air-raid when a bomb exploded nearby on the Embankment pavement. A large piece of stone was broken off its steps, and a hail of splinters pock-marked the pedestal and one of the bronze sphinxes. The scars are still visible, but barring an Act of God or the destructive powers of man, the Cleopatra's Needle can confidently look forward to many more centuries in this its final resting place.

Appendix

THE HIEROGLYPHIC INSCRIPTIONS

The Hieroglyphic language of the ancient Egyptians originated at some unknown date prior to 3,000BC, and its development was contemporary with—but separate from—the evolution of cuneiform writing by the Sumerians. The short description which follows is but a crude and simplified outline of the complex history of hieroglyphics, and if a more detailed account is desired the reader must resort to the various specialist works published on the subject. Initially the Egyptians merely used their hieroglyphs or picture symbols to represent the object portrayed, and they carved these pictographs in stone or painted them on plaster walls either to glorify one of their gods or to extol the attributes of a pharaoh. Gradually the meanings of some of the hieroglyphs were extended; firstly to help convey an associated idea and then later to help form part of a word which phonetically sounded similar. For instance a picture of an eye used in conjunction with other hieroglyphs produced a word or phrase connected with 'seeing', while the pictorial representation of a mouth eventually evolved into a purely phonetic symbol roughly equivalent to the modern letter R.

Originally hieroglyphics were solely devoted to inscriptions of a religious or royal nature on temples, tombs, obelisks and other structures, and because of this the complexity of the pictographs and the limitations of their meanings were not too serious a drawback, but as the Egyptian civilisation flourished the need arose for a simpler form of writing to enable records to be kept and documents of various kinds to be produced more easily. The first stage of this development was the Hieretic form with its simplified but still recognisable derivatives of the hieroglyphs which had been adapted for writing with a brush-pen on scrolls of papyrus. A later stage was the Demotic script which bears a resemblance to modern Arabic. Demotic script was probably evolved in the seventh century BC, and in time it completely superseded both its predecessors for all but certain religious inscriptions of a monumental nature. The last known use of the Hieroglyphic language occurred at the end of the fourth century AD, and after it fell into disuse all understanding of this form of writing was quickly lost to mankind. It was destined to remain a dead language for over one thousand years.

The French invaded Egypt in 1798, but although their occupation of the country was short lived—thanks to British intervention—one important outcome was the accidental discovery of the Rosetta Stone. In August 1799 while digging fortifications for Fort Saint Julien, some thirty miles east of Alexandria at the Rosetta mouth of the Nile, a French engineering officer named Boussard unearthed a polished slab of black basalt bearing an inscription written in three different languages: Hieroglyphic, Demotic, and Greek. General Menou rightly attached great importance to the find, and after ordering that the

64 The Rosetta Stone. Discovered in 1799 it bears in three languages a copy of the Decree of Memphis. The Rosetta Stone provided egyptologists with the key for rediscovering the long-dead hieroglyphic language.(From *Cleopatra's Needle* by J. King).

stone should be carefully cleaned he kept it in the safety of his tent. When Menou capitulated at Alexandria in 1801 the Rosetta Stone was surrendered to the British Commander-in-Chief who presented it to King George III, and the following year it was deposited in the British Museum. This broken slab of black basalt was destined to play the key role in unravelling the mysteries of the hieroglyphic inscriptions which decorate so many of the relics bequeathed to us by the ancient Egyptians.

The Rosetta Stone dates from around 195BC and it carried in three languages a copy of the Decree of Memphis with which the Egyptian priesthood honoured their ruler Ptolemy V. Its importance to the Egyptologists lay in the Greek version of the decree, for this enabled them at last to ascribe meanings to some of the symbols of the long dead Hieroglyphic language. An English scientist, Dr Thomas Young, successfully interpreted a few of the hieroglyphs, but it was the dedicated work of the Frenchman Jean Francois Champollion in the 1820s which provided a sure foundation for bringing back to life the many hieroglyphic inscriptions with which Egypt abounds. Champollion's task was not an

120

65 The Bankes Obelisk. It was brought to England and erected at Kingston Lacy, Dorset, in 1839, on a site chosen by the Duke of Wellington. Apart from Cleopatra's Needle it is the largest Egyptian obelisk domiciled in Britain. The Bankes Obelisk stands twenty-two feet high and weighs a mere six tons.

easy one, and even today after over a century and a half of painstaking study doubts still exist about the exact meanings of some of the hieroglyphs. Inscriptions were either written in vertical columns starting at the top or in horizontal rows, and although the latter were usually read from right to left this was by no means invariably the case. Each hieroglyph might be equivalent to a single letter of the Greek alphabet while on the other hand it could correspond to a group of letters, or it might have retained its original pictograph meaning and be merely a pictorial representation of an object or idea. These complications rendered the task of interpreting the symbols well-nigh impossible, and the foundation laid by Champollion's pioneering work were only slowly built upon by his successors. Further help was obtained from other multiple inscriptions, notably those on the Bankes Obelisk

FIRST SIDE.   SECOND SIDE.   THIRD SIDE.   FOURTH SIDE

66 The Hieroglyphic Inscriptions. A copy of the inscriptions on the four faces of the London needle. It was published in 1884.(From *Cleopatra's Needle* by J. King).

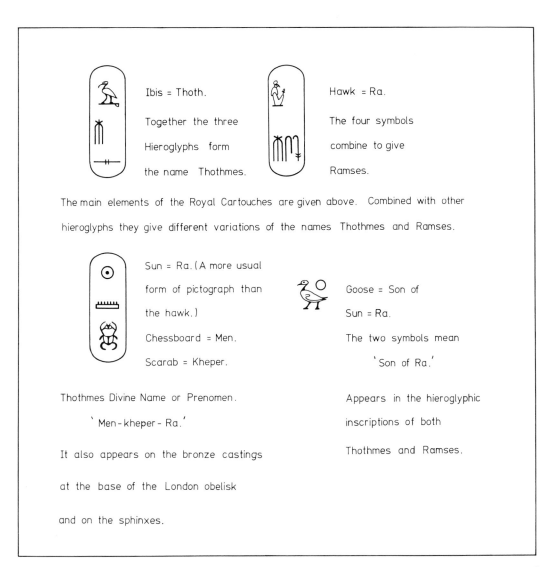

Ibis = Thoth.

Together the three

Hieroglyphs form

the name Thothmes.

Hawk = Ra.

The four symbols

combine to give

Ramses.

The main elements of the Royal Cartouches are given above. Combined with other hieroglyphs they give different variations of the names Thothmes and Ramses.

Sun = Ra. (A more usual form of pictograph than the hawk.)

Chessboard = Men.

Scarab = Kheper.

Goose = Son of Sun = Ra.

The two symbols mean 'Son of Ra.'

Thothmes Divine Name or Prenomen. 'Men-kheper-Ra.'

It also appears on the bronze castings at the base of the London obelisk and on the sphinxes.

Appears in the hieroglyphic inscriptions of both Thothmes and Ramses.

67 Details of the hieroglyphs. The details shown appear on both Cleopatra's Needles, although in the case of the New York obelisk they face the opposite way.

which now resides at Kingston Lacy in Dorset, and a stone discovered in 1866 bearing a copy of the Decree of Canopus.

To the ancient Egyptians the obelisk represented their supreme deity—the sun, from which the pharaohs considered themselves to be directly descended. The London and New York obelisks were erected around 1,450BC by the pharaoh Thothmes III to adorn the entrance of the Temple of the Sun at Heliopolis a few miles north-east of modern Cairo, and since they formed a matching pair with many of the hieroglyphics duplicated on both needles, the meanings of their inscriptions will be considered jointly. Both obelisks are inscribed with three vertical columns of hieroglyphics on each of their four tapering sides, the centre column in every instance being the original inscription dedicated to Thothmes III, while the flanking columns were added two hundred years later to glorify

Ramses II. The four sloping faces of each pyramidion are also inscribed. At the top of each column of hieroglyphs is a falcon, the symbolic representation of Horus the Egyptian god who ruled the earth. Immediately below in a rectangular box Horus is described as a mighty bull and King of Upper and Lower Egypt. The inscriptions also contain oval scrolls or cartouches containing various versions of the names of Thothmes and Ramses.

The name Thothmes means 'born of Thoth', the Egyptian god of wisdom and letters, who is represented in the hieroglyphics by an ibis (a wading bird worshipped by the ancient Egyptians), but references also occur to Thothmes being the son of, or descended from, other gods, namely the Sun God Ra, the mighty Horus, and Tem who was closely associated with Heliopolis. The central inscription clearly states that the pair of obelisks was erected at Heliopolis on the orders of Thothmes, and that their pyramidions were capped with electrum—a gold alloy. Reference is also made to his victories extending Egypt's frontiers, and the remainder of the inscriptions is devoted to his titles and ancestry. The flanking hieroglyphics added by Ramses II are less informative, and while recording his prowess as a warrior they do so in a vainer manner, and these inscriptions are mainly concerned with extolling the virtues of Ramses in rather exotic terms.

The hieroglyphics were inscribed with loving care by the skilled Egyptian masons in *intaglio relievo*—that is, they stand out from a recessed surface so that the tops of the symbols are flush with the outside faces of the obelisk. The hieroglyphics on the London needle are more or less complete thanks to the centuries during which it lay buried on the shore of the Mediterranean, but due to the American needle's longer exposure to wind-borne sand two of its faces have been seriously eroded and some of the hieroglyphs are undecipherable. In their new settings the two Cleopatra's Needles are safe from such erosion, but only time will tell whether or not atmospheric pollution and the colder damp climate they are now subjected to will prove equally harmful to their hieroglyphic inscriptions.

Bibliography and References

Information is given in two forms: firstly a short list of the major books and periodical articles consulted, followed by, on a chapter basis, exact references for the quotations cited.

(a) Select Bibliography

Unless stated otherwise the items concerned were published in London.

Alexander, J. E., *Cleopatra's Needle, the Obelisk of Alexandria, its acquisition etc.*, 1879

Baker, B., 'Cleopatra's Needle,' *Proceedings of the Institution of Civil Engineers*, vol. 61, (1879-80)

Budge, E. A., *Cleopatra's Needle and other Egyptian Obelisks*, 1926

Cooper, B. H., 'Cleopatra's Needle,' *The Graphic*, vol 17 (1878)

Cooper, W. R., *A Short History of the Egyptian Obelisks*, 1877

Dixon, J., 'On the Arrangements made for the Removal and for the Transport to England of Cleopatra's Needle,' *Journal of the Royal United Service Institution*, vol 21 (1877)

Engelbach, R., *The Problem of the Obelisks*, 1923

Farman, E. E., 'The Negotiations for the Obelisk,' *The Century Magazine*, vol 24 (1882), New York

Gorringe, H. H., *Egyptian Obelisks*, 1885

Iversen, E., *Obelisks in Exile*, Copenhagen 1972

King, J., *Cleopatra's Needle, a History of the London Obelisk*, 1883

Lebas, J. B. A., *L'Obelisque de Luxor*, Paris 1839

Wilson, E., (1), *Our Egyptian Obelisk, Cleopatra's Needle*, 1877

   (2), *Cleopatra's Needle*, 1878

(b) References

CHAPTER 1

1 *The Athenaeum*, 22 September 1877

2 Cooper, B. H., 114

3 Wilson (2), 187

4 *All the Year Round*, vol 1 (1859), 562

5 *The Engineer*, vol 45 (1878), 119

6 Titmarsh, M. A., *Notes on a Journey from Cornhill to Grand Cairo*, 1846, 224

7 Cooper, W., 130

8 Quoted in *The Illustrated London News*, 21 June 1851

9 *All the Year Round*, vol 1 (1859), 562

10 MacGregor, J., *The Rob Roy on the Jordan, etc.*, 1870, 69

CHAPTER 2

1 Alexander, 14

2 *Ibid*, 15

3 *Ibid*

4 *Ibid*, 17

5 *Ibid*, 25

6 *Ibid*, 29

7 *Newcastle Weekly Chronicle*, 1 February 1878
8 *Ibid*
9 *The Times*, 24 May 1875
10 Dixon, 1119
11 *Ibid*
12 Cooper, W., 140
13 *Ibid*, 141
14 Baker, 236
15 *Ibid*

CHAPTER 3
1 *The Times*, 24 May 1877
2 Alexander, 72
3 The letter was reprinted in *The Times* on 24 May 1877
4 Alexander, 74
5 *Engineering*, vol 24 (1877), 230
6 Baker, 237
7 *The Engineer*, vol 44 (1877), 211
8 *Ibid*
9 Dixon, 1121
10 *Engineering*, vol 24 (1877), 230
11 *The Engineer*, vol 44 (1877), 211
12 *Engineering*, vol 24 (1877), 230

CHAPTER 4
1 Baker, 240
2 Alexander, 83
3 Wilson (1), vii
4 *The Times*, 27 October 1877
5 Alexander, 81
6 *The Times*, 19 October 1877
7 *Ibid*
8 *Ibid*
9 *Ibid*
10 *Ibid*

CHAPTER 5
1 Baker, 242
2 Alexander, 89
3 *The Times*, 22 January 1878
4 *The Illustrated London News*, 26 January 1878

CHAPTER 6
1 *The Times*, 27 September 1877
2 *Ibid*
3 *The Times*, 31 January 1878
4 *Ibid*, 31 May 1878

5 *Ibid*, 13 June 1878
6 *Ibid*, 13 September 1878
7 Alexander, 100
8 *Engineering*, vol 26 (1878), 219
9 *The Times*, 13 September 1878
10 *Ibid*

CHAPTER 7
1 Gorringe, 2
2 Farman, 682
3 *The Times*, 19 November 1879
4 *Journal of the British Archaeological Association*, vol 33 (1877), 496
5 Gorringe, 11
6 *Ibid*, 15
7 *Ibid*, 28

CHAPTER 8
1 *The Academy*, vol 18 (1880), 88
2 *The Engineer*, vol 46 (1878), 265
3 *The Illustrated London News*, 21 September 1878

Index